Inquiring in the Classroom

Also available from Continuum

Conducting Research in Educational Contexts, Tehmina N. Basit
Effective Action Research, Patrick J. M. Costello
Reflective Teaching (3rd edition), Andrew Pollard
Researching Education, David Scott and Robin Usher

Inquiring in the Classroom

Asking the questions that matter about teaching and learning

Nick Mitchell
and
Joanne Pearson

continuum

Continuum International Publishing Group

The Tower Building	80 Maiden Lane
11 York Road	Suite 704
London SE1 7NX	New York NY 10038

www.continuumbooks.com

British Library Cataloguing-in-Publication Data
A catalogue record for this book is available from the British Library.

ISBN: 978-1-4411-5282-4 (paperback)
      978-1-4411-8237-1 (hardcover)

Library of Congress Cataloging-in-Publication Data
A catalog record of this book is available from the Library of Congress.

Typesetted by Deanta Global Publishing Services, Chennai, India
Printed and bound in Great Britain

This book is dedicated to the late Harry Corbett who taught us everything we know about team work and to all of our fabulous students who teach us as much as we teach them.

Contents

List of Contributors

Nick Mitchell is a Senior Lecturer in Education at Leeds Metropolitan University, UK. He was a science teacher for many years. In 1981 his school report said that 'his written work is lethargic, reflecting his natural laziness'.

Joanne Pearson is a Senior Lecturer in Education at Leeds Metropolitan University, UK, having previously been a secondary history teacher. She does an uncanny impersonation of Cary Grant.

Melanie Garlick is Inclusion Coordinator at a primary school in Huddersfield, UK, and is currently completing her Masters in special needs education. Mel's favourite biscuits are dark chocolate Hobnobs.

Katie Hall is a Senior Lecturer at Leeds Metropolitan University, UK, and has been working in teacher education for the past six years, having previously taught science and been Head of Year in a number of different secondary schools. Katie is one of the few people known to have discovered Fox's Glacier Dark sweets.

Barbara Hibbert is a freelance educational consultant, UK, producing online history teaching resources for the Prince's Teaching Institute and Teach First. She appeared on various TV quiz shows, most recently *Eggheads*, where she was knocked out in the history round – but only after going to sudden death.

Brendan Higgins is a postgraduate tutor in the School of Education at the University of Leeds, UK. He has 29 years experience in secondary education and is a former headteacher.

Matt Homer is a research fellow working in the Schools of Education and Medicine at the University of Leeds, UK. Most of his research is assessment-related, and he has published many articles with a quantitative slant in a range of education journals. Matt simply loves The Fall.

Cath Lawes is Inclusion Manager at a large high school in Leeds, UK, where she also teaches maths. Cath loves cycling and the Leeds Rhinos.

Erica Mace is a specialist support teacher having taught for 21 years throughout the primary school age range. Both of Erica's names are plant related.

Dean Pearson is Head of Social Sciences at a school in West Yorkshire, UK, where he teaches children across the 11–18 age range, and has 26 years' teaching experience. He plays the bass guitar and likes Sports Mixture but they have to be Lions ones.

Ian Price is Assistant Headteacher at a large comprehensive school in Yorkshire, UK, where he has, for several years, supported continuing professional development for beginning and experienced teachers. Ian once had his legs waxed for charity.

Jayne Price is music education coordinator, MTL course leader and MA tutor in the School of Education and Professional Development at the University of Huddersfield, UK. Jayne has a pet hamster.

Claire E. Smith is History PGCE tutor and the PGCert Module tutor at Leeds Trinity University College, UK. Claire is not in The Fall.

Louise Tracey is a research fellow in the Institute for Effective Education at the University of York, UK, and previously worked as a researcher in the School of Education's Centre for Teaching and Learning at the University of Nottingham, UK. At the age of 7 Louise's budgie disappeared up the Hoover (and survived!).

Fiona Woodhouse is a Senior Lecturer in Science Education at the University of Huddersfield, UK, and previously taught science in secondary schools. Fiona owns the most affectionate cat in England.

Foreword

We have written this book because teachers need to be helped to value their own ideas. After many years in which we as a profession have been told the answers to perennial issues in teaching, we feel it is time for teachers to be empowered to inquire into what is important to them and to find answers for themselves. That is why we have subtitled this book 'Asking the Questions that Matter'.

Although we knew there were excellent books around on classroom research, we felt none of them quite met the needs of all our students. In particular, these texts seemed to us to describe admirably how to carry out an inquiry in the classroom but without really explaining why teachers would ever want to do this. Reading some of these books could make classroom inquiry sometimes sound about as inviting as root canal surgery!

We are also aware that for some of you tackling teacher inquiry, the thought of additional work and, even more horrifying, additional work that might be assessed by somebody else, is far from appealing. We hope in this book to convince you that good teacher inquiry can actually make your life easier because it will make your teaching better. You can't spend a lifetime just being the teacher: sometimes you need to be the learner.

We have drawn together a team of writers who between them have many years' experience of classroom practice, of teaching classroom practitioners and of supporting them in their inquiries. While it may be obvious reading this book that we have different approaches and experience, what unites us is a conviction that teachers should find out for themselves what works and share that knowledge with each other. If 'Izzy, wizzy, let's get busy' worked that would be fantastic, but it doesn't. It took hard work for us all to write the book and we can't promise it won't be hard work to change aspects of classrooms that you are unhappy with but teaching isn't easy. That's why you are so important when you do it well.

Acknowledgements

This is the first book we have written together and we both know it would never have happened without the support and encouragement of our families and the following people who have generously given their time. For that we should like to thank Neil Clephan, John Tomsett, Kay Courtnage and Karen Macdonald.

Introduction: Why Should Teachers Inquire and What Questions Should They Ask?

Joanne Pearson and Nick Mitchell

Chapter Outline

Introduction

We have both been teachers for much of our entire working lives: teachers of children and now teachers of adults. The only certainty we have about our practice as teachers of more than 20 years is that there is always more to learn. What we think we know about teaching can be built upon the flimsiest of foundations: we have to keep asking and trying to answer fundamental questions about ourselves as teachers. That is what this book is about: what kind of a teacher am I and how do I know?

Why does this matter? Firstly teaching is recognized as a reflective practice (Donald Schön 1983, 1987): a job in which thinking about what we do, both as we do it and after we do it, is essential. Secondly teaching has a profoundly moral dimension (Gary Fenstermacher and Virginia Richardson 2000): teachers work with children; our practice as teachers impacts upon others. If we stop asking these questions how are they going to be affected?

The question becomes: how can we inquire? This is our professional development, so how can we ensure that we ask good questions and provide good answers? Research suggests that the best professional development for teachers is coherent, sustained and centred around the needs of the teacher doing it and the institution in which they work (Michael Totterdell et al. 2004, Phillipa Cordingley et al. 2005, Chris Day et al. 2006). This book is designed to provide a framework that allows you to plan continuous professional development (CPD) that does all of these things. Each chapter leads you through ways of thinking, reading and researching about your own practice. Each chapter aims to help you to develop, improve and show you ways to share your knowledge about teaching and learning.

Thinking it through

- When was the last time you learnt something new about teaching or about yourself as a teacher?
- How did you learn it? In a taught sessions? From a book? From a pupil? A colleague? By yourself?
- What did you do about what you learnt?
- How did you share what you had learnt with others?

Finding the questions to ask

What matters in professional development for teachers? Who should decide what is developed and investigated? Whose questions should be answered? Inquiry is a process, but as Marilyn Cochran-Smith and Susan Lytle (2009) argue, it can also be seen as a stance; as a way of thinking, not just a way of doing. Teachers and teaching are subject to constant pressure to 'improve', to find 'best practice', then adopt it and disseminate it. There is an assumption that the 'magic sponge' that fixes all ills is out there somewhere and that if teachers could only be taught to use this sponge in the same way, more children will demonstrate the outcomes that league tables and decision makers, value. The troubles with this construct of teaching are threefold. Firstly, we the teachers are thereby cast as passive interpreters rather than active constructors of knowledge. Secondly, we teachers become the medium through which this 'official' view of the world is transmitted and finally, it is implied that all situations are the same: schools, children, teachers are all homogenous. There is, however, an alternative way to construct teacher inquiry:

- teachers as active questioners of the 'taken for granted assumptions' such as: 'league tables tell us how good a school is', 'National Curriculum levels are reliable and valid evidence about children';
- teachers as inquirers in particular settings that are local and different: the same question can produce different answers in different settings, there is no such thing as universal 'best practice';
- teachers as the drivers of change rather than the implementers of policy.

This is the vision of teacher inquiry that has motivated the writing of this book.

We want you to ask questions, we want you to find answers that make you a better teacher but we want these questions to be *your* questions. We suggest that there are few, if any, universal answers to the questions that really matter in teaching: 'best practice' may indeed be like a unicorn, a beautiful and alluring creature but one that ultimately is a myth.

Inquiry has a power to move beyond replicating or even critiquing existing educational structures, to be a catalyst for reconstituting and reconstructing educational beliefs and practices: be it on the scale of your own classroom and your own practice or on a much wider canvas. You will, we hope, sense our belief running right through this book that empowerment for you as a teacher lies with inquiring in the right way into the questions that matter. Let's start with those questions.

Asking big questions

One of the biggest questions of all for any teacher is 'why am I doing this?' So much of the practice of teachers can be routine that we never stop to consider the purpose of what it is we are doing: filling in spreadsheets of grades, just to take one example. Why are we doing this? What is this all about? You may be thinking of several answers right now: we are told to, we are being monitored as teachers, we need to monitor students' progress and so on. However, there are deeper underlying questions that you could be asking. What is the impact of grading in this way on me as a teacher, on my pupils? This is a question that is both critical in that you are questioning the taken for granted. It is at the same time a *transformative* question: 'if the impact of what I am being asked to do is negative, what can I do to change it?'

Have a look at the following questions about gender and race and consider the ways in which each question might involve you being more or less critical. For which questions is inquiry more a *process* and for which is inquiry more a *stance*?

1. How can boys achieve higher literacy levels?
2. How do boys experience literacy?
3. How do 'white' schools experience race through the curriculum?
4. Can peer coaching improve white working class attainment?

All of these questions are interesting: but some open up greater spaces than others for reconsidering and thinking through teaching as a practice and knowledge as a given. In question one, for example, the given is that the issue lies with the boys. The problem is that they underachieve. The implication is that we need to find the 'magic sponge' that fixes this problem. The second question in contrast, makes fewer assumptions: the boys are not the problem, but they may help us to find our way to an answer. Some questions make us think more because they require us to look at issues in new ways, such as the following: 'Are white working classes the problem or is the curriculum and the ways we record attainment the issue?'

How might you then discover and frame questions that are more critical, that open up larger areas for consideration, that make fewer assumptions; that matter more?

1. Chose areas of inquiry in which you are interested and for which you have some passion. You might go right back to some of your most fundamental reasons for becoming a teacher to find these areas. For example, when you first started out as a teacher, did you have a strong sense of social justice, of changing outcomes for disadvantaged pupils? How could this help you to frame questions in order to explore whether these aims are still evident and embedded in your practice or that of your current school?

   These might be inquiries that investigate where you currently are: *what aspirations do working class girls have in our school? Do children on free school meals (FSM) achieve in my lessons? Do SEN children feel included in my classroom?* Exploring these kinds of questions can often lead you towards confronting larger and less immediately obvious themes.

   There are also questions that help you to evaluate the ways in which you are tackling an issue that has already been identified. *Why aren't more FSM pupils opting for the English Baccalaureate? Why don't more pupils from disadvantaged backgrounds participate in extracurricular activities? How can pupils with ADHD be supported more effectively in maths?*

Lastly there are questions that evaluate the efficacy of any interventions you may have adopted to tackle a concern. *Is mixed ability setting raising the aspirations of working class girls? Is the reading recovery scheme working over the medium and long term? Has the buddy system made pupils with SEN feel more included in school?*

2. Inquire into areas that trouble or concern you. As teachers we can often be asked, for example, to implement policy that we hold reservations about; sometimes these policies are at a national level and sometimes they are at a school or local level. The National Curriculum assessment tests (SATs) would be a good example of such a policy. If inquiry is just a process then perhaps we could argue that inquiring into the impact of SATs on pupils and on teaching is pointless; others have done it (the Cambridge Primary Review 2009 being one of the most recent) and the tests remain, but if we accept inquiry as stance then these kinds of questions and challenges still matter.

   If teachers stop asking the questions, producing the evidence and trying to convince parents and policy makers then we are absolving ourselves of our professional responsibility. It is our role to keep challenging the things that trouble us as teachers.

   Policies that are of concern might not always come from a national level; Key Stage 3 assessment tests are a good example here. These tests are no longer compulsory but many schools still use them to provide the only summative assessment for pupils at the end of the Key Stage. Examples of questions here could be the following. *Are optional SAT tests the most valid way to record summative assessment in Year 9 Maths? Are we teaching to the test in Year 9 Physics? Does testing in Year 9 English help pupils prepare for GCSE?*

   It may help you to frame questions like this in three phases. *Do we have a problem? How can we address a problem we have identified? Is our intervention/ innovation working?*

3. Inquire into issues that are of particular reference in the setting in which you work. Inquiry can give you a local perspective on issues that may or may not be of national significance. For example, in a school with a largely white mono-culture you may be interested in how children perceive race; in a school where there are few pupils with disabilities you may be interested in pupils' perceptions of disability. You might want to evaluate particular changes that you have made to your school or curriculum. *What are parents' and carers' perceptions of the way the school communicates with them? Do pupils in Year 4 enjoy the creative curriculum?*

4. Inquire into issues that are particularly of concern in your subject or Key Stage. The questions you choose might be exploratory. *Do children enjoy the books we have chosen for guided reading? How do African-Caribbean pupils feel about the history curriculum?* They might be diagnostic. *How can the PE curriculum better*

meet the needs of pupils with disabilities? How can topic work evidence attainment in the foundation subjects more effectively at Key Stage 2? Or they might be evaluative. *Is active learning in Science engaging more pupils? Is problem based learning in maths allowing pupils in lower sets to make progress?*

5. Inquire into issues as a response to research and reading. There is a lot written about teaching, much of it by people who are no longer as active in the classroom as you are (and that includes us by the way!). Their work is not just there to be used and read by other academics; it should inform and support practitioners. You might read a piece written by a fellow teacher in a professional journal, for example, and decide to explore the same question/topic because you are interested, because it sounds exciting or because you really don't agree with what they suggest and want to try this for yourself. For example, in February 2011, the journal of the National Association for English Teachers (www.nate.org.uk) explored teachers' reading practices. Studying this could lead to questions such as the following. *What do teachers read and how does this impact upon the curriculum? Do we have up to date knowledge about fiction for children in the English department?*

If you adopt the approach to inquiry that we have set out here, we warn you that you might find some unexpected or even uncomfortable answers. You might sometimes feel powerless to change aspects of teaching that seem not to be working but remain part of 'official' school or national policy. What we believe it can and we hope will do is to re-engage you in what you are doing and why. We both believe passionately that teaching can and should be an intensely intellectual pursuit.

One of the ways in which individuals can effect change within organizations and within professions is when they come together to look at common concerns. The day when you and your colleagues engage in classroom inquiry and talk to each other; share your findings, your methods and your recommendations will be the day that the orthodoxies of your practices begin to be challenged and made to justify themselves.

Thinking it through

- When you think about your practice do some issues immediately spring to mind? List them. How do they relate to the five areas outlines above? Are they based on your passions, your concerns, your current school?

⇨

- When did you last read about teaching? Or about new developments within a subject discipline. When did you last 'learn' or show a passion for learning? Research can seem intimidating and it has to be acknowledged that some of it is obliquely written to say the least, but much of the research on teaching is someone writing up their practice or that of others; it has lots to offer us.
- Can you identify other teachers in your setting or outside that you would like to work alongside in inquiring into practice? This is constructivism in action (see Chapter 4 for more discussion of this)

Ethics

Asking questions and collecting evidence to help you answer them can become a way of teaching. However, like teaching, inquiry also has a moral dimension. If you are registered on a university programme, your university will have its own ethical guidelines: the things you have to complete before collecting evidence from inside schools. This is more important than the bureaucratic process it may seem: inquiry can help and can harm, both those you study and you as the inquirer. There are therefore some key questions you need to consider before beginning any inquiry:

- Why do you want to investigate this? What are the benefits? For whom?
- What might be some of the risks of this inquiry? For whom?
- Do you have the permissions you need to undertake this research? From whom do you need permission?
- How could this inquiry impact upon your professional code of practice?

It might be quite useful to explore some examples at this point:

Thinking it through

Sally is a PE teacher; she wants to explore pupil enjoyment of Key Stage 3 PE. She decides to give her students a questionnaire.

Who should Sally get permission from for this inquiry? The head teacher? The parents? The pupils themselves?

⇨

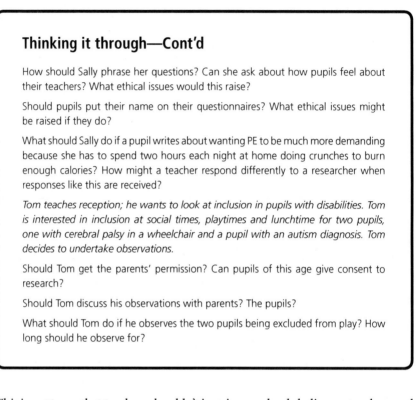

Thinking it through—Cont'd

How should Sally phrase her questions? Can she ask about how pupils feel about their teachers? What ethical issues would this raise?

Should pupils put their name on their questionnaires? What ethical issues might be raised if they do?

What should Sally do if a pupil writes about wanting PE to be much more demanding because she has to spend two hours each night at home doing crunches to burn enough calories? How might a teacher respond differently to a researcher when responses like this are received?

Tom teaches reception; he wants to look at inclusion in pupils with disabilities. Tom is interested in inclusion at social times, playtimes and lunchtime for two pupils, one with cerebral palsy in a wheelchair and a pupil with an autism diagnosis. Tom decides to undertake observations.

Should Tom get the parents' permission? Can pupils of this age give consent to research?

Should Tom discuss his observations with parents? The pupils?

What should Tom do if he observes the two pupils being excluded from play? How long should he observe for?

This is not to say that teachers shouldn't inquire; we clearly believe as teachers and authors that they should. We have included this section to show you that inquiry needs careful thought and lots of discussion. For those teachers working with a university on their inquiries, the first port of call should be the requirements of that university. For others the guidelines of the British Educational Research Association provide a comprehensive guide to ethical inquiry (BERA 2011).

Using this book

The book is designed to support all teachers; from early years to post 16, from main scale to leadership scale. It can be used as a support for formal accredited study at masters level and beyond or for teachers and schools who want to think about and change their practice for their own development and nothing more. You can read the book from cover to cover or dip into individual chapters and explore teaching in the order you choose. Most importantly from our perspective, the book is based upon ways of developing teachers that have been shown to work; not only in published research (Phillipa Cordingley et al. 2005, 2007) but in our own experiences as teachers and teacher educators. These can be summed up as:

- Activities that encourage teachers to inquire into their own practices and the practices within their school. Collecting evidence, analysing it, planning from it.
- Activities that encourage teachers to see a variety of evidence. Pupils' work, pupils' voices and opinions, lesson observations and plans, parents' feedback. In other words the stuff of everyday day teaching and life in a school. How can looking at it in different ways change things?
- Activities that encourage teachers to talk to each other and work together to find things out.
- Activities that are long term. There are few if any quick fixes in teaching. The chapters in this book encourage you to think about issues over more significant time spans and see the inquiries you undertake as cumulative, leading and informing each other.

Throughout the book you will find boxes marked 'thinking it through'. These contain questions to provoke and extend your thinking, suggestions for activities and ideas for involving colleagues in your inquiry. These boxes are there to help you ground your inquiries firmly in your school and practice as well as make them manageable, ethical and collaborative. These boxes might also point you towards opportunities to work with colleagues and to talk through what you are doing and why. Collaborative working, sharing your ideas and moving on together should always be an important part of teaching in a school or college. Some of the tasks in 'thinking it through' could make good discussion points in age phase, departmental or whole school meetings, others might spark off informal discussions at lunch or break time.

The book is divided into three sections. Part I explores some of the mechanics of good teacher inquiry. Asking questions without first establishing whether and how other people have asked them before would be a missed opportunity, so the section begins with reading for inquiry. How can teachers read critically? What kind of reading should they do? Chapter 2 introduces you to some of the important ideas in methodology; the tools that you will need to carry out your teacher inquiry. Chapter 3 then takes these methods into the classroom offering you practical advice on how to combine inquiry with your day job.

In Part II of the book we have examined four pillars of teaching: assessment, learning and teaching; subject knowledge; diversity and inclusion; leadership and management. The chapters in this section examine how to construct classroom inquiries in particular areas of teaching and learning. How can you examine your assessment practices to make them better? What makes a good curriculum for your children? How can you meet the needs of all pupils in your care? Are teaching assistants being used effectively in your classroom?

Are departmental policies working? Each chapter explores these kinds of questions, pointing you to key reading and previous research and then providing case studies that demonstrate how you, together with colleagues, would go about identifying a question, planning and structuring an inquiry, carrying it out and evaluating your data.

The final section of the book explores ways in which your professional development, your emerging data and your new knowledge can be shared your colleagues within and beyond your school.

The purpose of this book is to empower teachers at all levels to make themselves better teachers and ultimately provide a better education for children and young people. Your own professional development lies within reach; you just need to know how to start.

References

Alexander, R. (2009) *Children, their World, their Education: Final Report and Recommendations of the Cambridge Primary Review*. London: Routledge.

BERA (2011) *Revised Educational Guidelines for Educational Research*. Available at: www.bera.ac.uk (Accessed 12-Jun-11)

Cochran-Smith, M. and Lytle, S.L. (2009) *Inquiry as Stance: Practitioner Research for the Next Generation*. New York: Teachers College Press.

Cordingley, P., Bell, M., Thomason, S. and Firth, A. (2005) The impact of collaborative continuing professional development (CPD) on classroom teaching and learning. Review: How do collaborative and sustained CPD and sustained but not collaborative CPD affect teaching and learning? In: *Research Evidence in Education Library*. London: EPPI-Centre.

Cordingley, P., Bell, M., Isham, C., Evans, D. and Firth, A. (2007) What do specialists do in CPD programmes for which there is evidence of positive outcomes for pupils and teachers? Report. In: *Research Evidence in Education Library*. London: EPPI-Centre.

Cremin, T. (2011) Reading Teachers/Teaching Readers Why Teachers Who Read Make Good Teachers of Reading. *English, Drama and Media,* Vol. 19, pp. 11–18.

Day, D., Stobart, G., Sammons, P., Kington, A., Gu, Q., Smees, R., and Mujtaba, T. (2006) *Variations in Teachers' Work, Lives and Effectiveness*, London: Department for Education and Skills.

Fenstermacher, G. and Richardson, V. (2000) An Inquiry into the moral dimensions of teaching, in Poulson, L. and Wallace, M. (eds.) *Learning to Read Critically in Teaching and Learning*. Thousand Oaks: Sage.

Schön, D (1983). *The Reflective Practitioner: How Professionals Think in Action*. New York: Basic Books.

Schön, D (1987). *Educating the Reflective Practitioner*. San Francisco: Jossey-Bass.

Totterdell, M., Woodroffe, L., Bubb, S., and Hanrahan, K. (2004) *The Impact of NQT Induction Programmes on the Enhancement of Teacher Expertise, Professional Development, Job Satisfaction or Retention Rates: A Systematic Review of Research Literature on Induction*. London: EPPI Centre.

Part 1
The Tools of Teacher Inquiry

Reading for Teacher Inquiry

Jayne Price

Introduction

Reading the right literature is one of the most powerful ways to access the thoughts and practices of other teachers and educators. As teachers, we know how valuable it can be to learn from each other but most of us do not habitually access the wealth of accumulated knowledge on teaching that lies in thousands of books, journals and other articles. Look around your staff room and you will be lucky to find any books on 'teaching' at all. The only time we, as a profession generally read about our work is when we have to because we are taking a course. I hope in this chapter to play a small part in remedying this situation by showing you something of the potential of reading both as part of an inquiry but also as a professional development activity in its own right.

Reading is an essential component of any teacher inquiry and the quality of your engagement with literature will certainly be a major aspect of the assessment criteria if you are studying at masters level. Neil Denby et al. (2008) argue that the ability to relate your own work to wider professional frameworks is essential for developing 'mastery' of your professional practice. Reading what other people have written about your inquiry focus will build your knowledge and understanding of the topic and help you to locate your work within this wider context. Judith Bell suggests that:

> In a small scale project, you will not be expected to produce a definitive account of the state of research in your selected topic area, but you will need to provide evidence that you have read a certain amount of literature and that you have some awareness of the current state of knowledge.
>
> Bell (2005, 33)

Reading in the early stages of your study, as you are exploring the focus and refining your inquiry question is important as this will help you to develop a rationale for your work. As your understanding of the prior research and existing knowledge within your focus area grows, you may discover areas of controversy, identify links with your own practice that you want to explore, or uncover aspects that need further explanation. All of these can help shape your own inquiry. You might also identify data collection methods that could prove helpful, or you might refine your ideas about how to classify and present your own data. As we suggest elsewhere in this book, 'borrowing' methodology from other authors is a perfectly acceptable practice.

Of course, ongoing reading throughout your study will be just as important. As you are analysing your evidence and reflecting on your own practice, this will spark questions that you will want to explore further in the literature and this in turn will deepen your analysis and help you to make recommendations or identify areas for further development. Developing your ability to synthesize theory and practice in this way is a major part of working at masters level but it's equally a powerful tool for professional development.

Finally, in this section, some words of motivation. Many students are daunted by the volume of reading that is necessary to produce a good assignment or account of an inquiry. Naturally, much of what you need to read is not the sort of material you would choose yourself: nobody (I hope!) reads this sort of literature for pleasure. All I can say to reassure you is that in my experience you would be an unusual student if you did not look back one day with satisfaction on what you will have read and mastered as a result of writing about your inquiries in the classroom. That is not to forget either the pleasure that comes from thinking about your practice, using your brain again, tackling the questions that really matter to you or being able to counter the arguments of your headteacher or your chair of governors by quoting research back at her!

When to read?

That still leaves you needing to fit this reading into your busy life. The answer depends on how you learn best: some people need to lock themselves away for a weekend to read and make notes, others can spread their work over evenings and lunchtimes. In fact one of the first and most challenging tasks when you start a course can be to reinvent yourself as a student: 'Just how do I learn best?'

As teachers, we have a great resource which will help us here. As our 'day job' we help people learn, so we're quite good at thinking about how to help others to do pretty much what we are now being asked to do. So think, 'how would you help a child read?' Use the same strategies on yourself. Break the task down, so you read a page or two, maybe a section of an article then have a break and allow your mind time to process the information. Reward yourself for completing a difficult article or chapter. Extend yourself when you feel you are sailing through a text by being particularly critical of what you are reading. You know the sort of strategies I mean.

So what I'm really suggesting here is that even if you are an 'all in one go' person, you break reading down and do bits at lunchtime, before you go to sleep, at weekends, whatever works for you. You need to let this literature become a part of your life, for a while at least. It will go away again: but by then you'll be a better practitioner.

What to read?

Being selective about what you read will be necessary in order to keep within the time constraints of your study. There are a wide variety of sources available: 'literature' can be anything from an article in an academic journal to a comment on a website and part of adopting a critical approach is recognizing that some sources have more credibility than others.

Journals

An article in an academic journal is considered to be the most credible source of information as the process of peer review ensures that only the best articles are selected for publication. These often report on the author's research and the claims made will have been scrutinized before publication by other experts in the field. Don't be surprised or disheartened if you find reading journal articles like this difficult at first. The ideas in them may be difficult or unfamiliar and they are often written in what might seem like an unnecessarily opaque style. You will find reading these articles easier with practice and if you follow the advice on active reading below.

Articles in professional journals (like, for example, *The Teacher*: www. teachers.org.uk; and *Teaching Today*: www.nasuwt.org.uk) may also be peer reviewed but are judged more on their usefulness for practice rather than their 'academic' quality. These often contain strong opinions and political comment which may help you to substantiate a critique of current policy. Both academic and professional journal articles are likely to be more 'current' than books which can take up to two years to get from proposal to publication.

Books

Authored books and single chapters in edited books allow for extended discussion about a topic and reading these will develop your knowledge and understanding of the inquiry focus. You will be able to identify recurring themes or aspects that form the basis of current knowledge in the field and reading widely will enable you to compare and contrast different authors' views. Be wary of citing evidence in your assignment from textbooks, which may be very useful in providing an initial overview of a topic, but generally contain an interpretation of other authors' work which may or may not be an accurate summary. Always try to go back to the original source to help you develop a more informed argument.

Websites

Websites are potentially the most problematic sources of information. The claims made are not subject to any review process and they can contain misleading or unsubstantiated opinion. When you do find useful information, it can be difficult to attribute it and an assignment full of web references is unlikely to be well received by your tutor. However, many sites offer access to electronic versions of published material, also the vast majority of educational policy literature is published online: accessing this will help you understand the full context of your area of study. The subject associations (e.g., National Association for the Teaching of English: www.nate.org.uk; the Mathematical Association: www.m-a.org.uk) and other sites such as charities (e.g., the Sutton Trust: www.suttontrust.com) and think tanks (e.g., DEMOS: www.demos. co.uk) can also be rich sources of ideas.

Louise Poulson and Mike Wallace (2004) identify three different types of knowledge expressed in the literature described above – theoretical knowledge, research knowledge and practice knowledge. Theoretical knowledge is generated through reflection on an aspect of the social world; the author develops a set of concepts to explain a particular phenomenon. Research knowledge is based on empirical investigation; the claims made are supported by evidence and analysis. Practice knowledge is derived from the interpretation and evaluation of classroom practice.

There are strong links between these types of knowledge and Poulson and Wallace (2004) acknowledge that many texts reflect more than one. For example, theory is often derived from the empirical testing of a hypothesis; practice knowledge is often supported by empirical inquiry. All three types of knowledge are generally concerned with the development and improvement of practice. But Poulson and Wallace suggest that identifying the type of knowledge underpinning the writing helps us to critically reflect on the potential limitations of the author's claims, such as considering the potential flaws in the methodology used to develop research based knowledge; questioning the generalizability of claims in practice-based knowledge or potentially identifying a lack of evidence to support a developed theory.

It is this recognition that the written word might not always be a 'true' reflection of reality; that explanations of the social world are never definitive and always open to question or competing interpretation that forms the basis of demonstrating the ability to be 'critical' in your assignment.

Criticality

Being 'critical' is essential for successful masters level study and indeed, for pursuing any inquiry rigorously and you need to develop an understanding of what this means, and practise reading, thinking and writing critically in order to get better at it. Being critical is about adopting a sceptical stance when reading: your aim should be to think objectively about a topic, to consider the points raised and the evidence presented, to evaluate it and compare it with your own experience and essentially to develop your own opinion. Your ability to do this is demonstrated in the way you write about both previous research and your own data in your assignment.

Jennifer Moon (2008) considers various definitions of criticality collected during her research with higher education tutors: one that sums up my thoughts about critical thinking in this context particularly well is:

> Critical thinking is the ability to consider a range of information derived from many different sources, to process this information in a creative and logical manner, challenging it, analysing it and arriving at considered conclusions which can be defended and justified.
>
> Moon (2008, 30)

The following processes will help you to develop a critical approach to your study and also incidentally help direct you towards questioning the things that really matter:

- Consider the context: this might mean the local, national, cultural contexts or how the work sits within a broader argument or within a theoretical framework.
- Question meanings and the definitions of the terms you see used, look for and acknowledge underlying assumptions. As an example of this, you can read a discussion around the term 'inclusion' in Chapter 7 of this book.
- Evaluate evidence, be sceptical and recognize possible limitations in terms of generalizability: in other words how might what you are reading be applied to other contexts such as the one you're investigating?
- Consider the relationship of the work to others that you have read, highlight areas of agreement and conflict between different authors.
- Keep focused, purposeful and precise; adopting a critical approach involves being aware of your own thinking processes.

Thinking it through

Practise the processes outlined above by thinking critically about the following statement made by the Michael Gove during his speech at the 2011 NCSL conference on the moral purpose of education.

'An outstanding school will look after the pastoral needs of its pupils; will provide a wide range of extra-curricular activities, and play a role as a broader part of its community. But it must also endow each child with the basic entitlement of intellectual capital any citizen needs to make their way in the world. A GCSE floor standard is about providing a basic minimum expectation to young people that their school will equip them for further education and employment'.

⇨

How are your responses to this statement affected by your own school context?

Which terms need further explanation or definition?

What do you think are the underlying assumptions and values inherent in the statement?

How do you feel your own values affect your responses to the statement?

What are possible alternative viewpoints?

Critical reading

For non-critical readers, sources provide 'facts' and the purpose of reading is to absorb these facts in order to develop an understanding of the topic under investigation. Non-critical readers are most interested in identifying the main points raised in the text and their writing about that literature is likely to consist of little more than restatement and summaries of what different authors have said. Critical readers on the other hand recognize that a source contains only *one* version of the facts and that in order to gain a full understanding, the text must be interrogated, the reasoning and evidence provided must be evaluated and the author's values and perspectives taken into to account. In their writing they use literature to develop a coherent argument and their writing is characterized by interpretation, evaluation, comparison and contrast of alternative viewpoints and synthesis.

Critical reading requires a much more 'active' approach to engaging with literature; a conscious effort to look for inner meanings and underlying assumptions and to question the evidence presented by the author.

You might start by thinking about the authority of the author: who are they? Are they writing from a theoretical perspective, are they presenting evidence from a research project or are they writing from their own practical experience? You also need to think about the time relevance of the work. It is generally accepted that in an academic assignment you should be looking at literature which is no more than 10 years old, unless the work is particularly influential in nature or you are presenting the focus from a historical perspective. Does the work reflect current policy and practice?

Next you need to identify the claims the author is making and the evidence they provide to make these claims. Consider the author's tone and their use of persuasive argument; is the evidence strong or weak? Are the examples used to explain ideas credible? If the writing is based on empirical data, what are the threats to validity and reliability (you will find these two terms defined in the next chapter)? Does the author consider exceptions to their claims? What might these be? Do the conclusions the author makes follow logically from the arguments and evidence provided?

Thinking it through

Critically evaluate the following text taken from *Pedagogy and Practice: Teaching and Learning in Secondary Schools, Unit 19: Learning Styles*, published by the DfES in 2004.

In any one classroom there will be different groups of learners whose engagement and understanding will be supported by different sorts of learning opportunities. If you want to get the best out of all your pupils, it is important to have an understanding of their preferred learning styles. You can then use that understanding to make them aware of their own learning preferences as well as to plan and deliver appropriate learning activities.

Research indicates that in general 35 per cent of people are mainly visual learners, 40 per cent of people are mainly kinaesthetic and only 25 per cent are mainly auditory.

Many schools systematically compile information on pupils' preferred learning styles and use it to inform their lesson planning and classroom management. There are two main methods by which the data can be collected: questionnaires and teacher observation. Each has equal validity and you might choose the one you feel most comfortable with or use both to check results.

A visual learner prefers to read, to see the words, illustrations and diagrams; talks quite fast, using lots of images; memorizes by writing repeatedly; when inactive, looks around, doodles or watches something; when starting to understand something says, 'that looks right'; is most distracted by untidiness.

An auditory learner likes to be told, to listen to the teacher, to talk it out; talks fluently, in a logical order, and with few hesitations; memorizes by repeating words aloud; when inactive, talks to self or others; when starting to understand something says, 'that sounds right'; is most distracted by noises. A kinaesthetic learner likes to get involved, hands on, to try it out; uses lots of hand movements; talks about actions and feelings; speaks more slowly; memorizes by doing something repeatedly; when inactive, fidgets, walks around; when starting to understand something says, 'that feels right'; is most distracted by movement or physical disturbance.

DfES
(2004, 4–5)

⇨

Consider the purpose of the writing.

What are the main claims made in the extract?

How are they reasoned or argued for?

What evidence is provided to support the claims made and how do you evaluate this?

What do other authors say about the claims?

How does this extract compare with your own practice?

Voice

The whole point about reading in this way is that it helps you to develop your own opinion and your writing about literature will be stronger if you can allow your own 'voice' to come through. Some students find it difficult to assert the confidence to do this, deferring instead to the perceived authority of more 'academic' or published authors. Remember, however, that as a teacher you have practical experience of working as a professional, you have worked with learners with a wide age and ability range and are constantly engaged in dialogue with colleagues. This experience is more than enough to give you the authority to question any authors' assertions about practice.

Active reading

Actively reading, thinking about critical questions and making notes on these as you read, will enable you to develop the sort of notes that will be helpful for you when you start to plan your assignment. There are lots of ways of doing this and you will need to find a system that works for you, but the following ideas have been found useful by my students working on masters level projects.

- Use different colours to identify and highlight recurring themes in the literature. Highlighting can be done on your initial first read through a source in order to identify underlying themes, then you could start to make notes separately for each theme. This will help you to synthesize the work of authors who are making similar claims.

- Try using a table with two columns to write notes when you find contrasting opinions in the literature. This will help you to develop a balanced argument in your work.
- As you make notes about the claims the author is making, choose a different colour to comment on different aspects of what you are reading. For example, identifying issues with the evidence provided, noting questions the text raises, links to other sources you have read, how the ideas might work in practice, or how you could use the source in your assignment.
- After reading a source, while it is still fresh in your mind, write a summary of the main points in your own words. In this way, as you are writing notes you are already starting to write part of your inquiry. The beauty of doing this on a computer is that you can adapt it, move it about and refine it later.

Thinking it through

Sharing your ideas about the literature is a good way to consolidate your understanding and develop a critical response to a source. When a group of you are working on the same focus, it is a good opportunity to work together in this way. Start by each taking one source to work on in detail; develop some notes about what the text says and your reactions to it. Write a critical summary in your own words to share with the others in the group. Together, compare and contrast the different sources you have looked at, identifying areas of consensus and conflict.

Writing about literature in your inquiry

Depending on the reason why you are undertaking your classroom inquiry, you might have to write a full literature review or you may be writing a shorter account of your inquiry. The advice that follows is intended to cover all sorts of inquiries, especially since the same criteria for writing critically about literature apply equally to the very shortest or the very longest reviews of literature.

Once you have read this section, you might also wish to refer to Chapter 10 which is about writing and presenting your inquiry.

As I have argued, we need to approach literature in a discursive style in assignments rather than presenting summaries of what other people have said about the topic one after the other. Remember that your aim should be to show your engagement with the literature. Neil Denby et al. (2008) urge us to adopt a 'theme by theme' approach rather than a 'source by source' approach. In this way you will tend to debate and contrast themes rather than simply describe and list what you've read. As you are reading, underlying themes around your topic will be emerging: in sketching these out you are starting to develop a theoretical framework for your inquiry. Outlining the underlying themes and how they are connected is a good place to start the introduction to your review of the literature you have read.

Structure

Writing your literature review is like being a conductor leading the orchestra in a performance of a classical symphony. The piece starts with the introduction and the major themes of the work are presented. Here is the chance to set the scene, to introduce the melodies that will be developed later to the audience. In your assignment, start by outlining the focus generally and then introduce the main themes that you will discuss in the literature review; how they characterize your focus and why they are important. Gary Thomas (2009) suggests that you should try to build interest in the focus by establishing the 'trouble' or areas of controversy, the issues, questions or uncertainties.

In the middle section of the piece, themes are developed; different instruments of the orchestra are highlighted and used for their dramatic effect, sometimes playing in unison; sometimes in harmony, sometimes concordant; sometimes dissonant. Contrasting themes are presented and tensions are exposed and explored, but always with a sense of direction and within a coherent structure. At this point in the review, you will need to outline the different arguments you have found in the literature, synthesize the work of different authors and offer your analysis of the issues raised.

In the concluding section of the symphony, the main themes are restated and summarized, often presented in a slightly different way after their development during the middle section of the piece, but always recognizable as the original themes of the piece. Here you need to summarize the main points you have explored during the review, outlining the major contributions from different authors. You will want to highlight any questions that still remain unresolved and finally and perhaps most importantly, consider the links to your own inquiry.

Thinking it through

After reading a lot of literature, you often can't see the wood for the trees! One way to help you establish a flow and a direction is to try to explain what you've found to somebody else who knows little about the topic. A non-teaching partner is ideal as having to explain what you're writing in non-specialist language will help concentrate your mind and help you improve the coherence of what you finally write.

Case study: Developing analysis strategies in a literature review

In this case study, Parveen conducted an inquiry entitled 'Is my assessment fit for purpose?' She focused particularly on developing her written and verbal feedback for a Year 10 Religious Education group. She used the following strategies throughout her literature review to demonstrate her engagement with the literature and to analyse the issues underpinning her focus.

- *Restatement* – Outlining what the text says using a mixture of direct quotation, paraphrase and summary.

  Direct quotations are used when the author makes a clear statement that you feel is important enough to repeat word for word. *Paraphrasing* involves explaining a passage from an author in your own words. *Summarizing* is where you outline the main points from a source. The following example from Parveen's assignment paraphrases Ruth Dann's (2002) comments about the dominance of the use of assessment to measure progress against predetermined objectives.

  > It has been recognised that as a product of the National Curriculum's measurement dominant model, a culture of measuring against objectives has become standard practice in state schools (Dann, 2002). Dann argues that as a direct result of this, schools in England are more immersed in a measurement paradigm of assessment rather than an inquiry paradigm.

- *Description* – Outlining what the text does, as well as what is says.

  In this example, Parveen describes the juxtaposition of formative and summative assessment by Paul Black and Dylan Wiliam (1998) and the further critique offered by Chris Watkins (2003).

  > Black & Wiliam (1998) highlighted the clash between the two key systems of summative and formative assessment, recognising that they both served a purpose but that the current education system's over reliance on summative assessment was detrimental. Others have gone further, arguing that the term assessment has been hijacked, no longer referring to the process of drawing out student learning (Watkins, 2003).

- *Interpretation* – Outlining the meaning of the text but in your own terms.

  In this example Parveen writes about the significance of Black and Wiliam's 'Inside the Black Box'.

  > Before Black and Wiliam's *Inside the Black Box* (1998), it seems that formative assessment was thought of by many teachers as at best a novelty, at worst an irrelevance. Many had not even considered that what they were doing in their everyday teaching was 'formative assessment'.

- *Synthesis* – Recognition that different sources are making the same or similar claims or arguments.

  Here, Parveen combines the work of Caroline Gipps et al (2000), the Assessment Reform Group (2002), Shirley Clarke (2001) and Eleanore Hargreaves (2005) to argue that the most effective feedback is a two-way process.

  > Findings from the Assessment Reform Group (2002) suggest that the best feedback is that which leads to students recognising their next steps and how to take them. Hargreaves (2005) is in agreement with this statement but sees this as a joint recognition for both the teacher and the learner of where the learning is heading next. This theme is echoed in the work of Gipps et al (2000) and Clarke (2002) who argue that for assessment to be truly 'formative' the information from assessments must feed back in to the teaching process, helping teachers plan the next appropriate teaching episode for the individual learner.

- *Contrast* – A balanced argument is presented by contrasting the different views inherent within the literature.

  In this example, Parveen highlights differences of opinion about graded and 'comment only' marking.

There is some debate over what form the feedback should take. It has been recognised that the teacher's judgement is important to indicate the level of achievement; Harry Torrance (2001) maintains that this is needed to form a reference point for both peer and self-assessment. Others argue that feedback should consist of 'comment only' marking, highlighting only the positive qualities of the student's work and advice on what they can do to improve (Black and Wiliam, 1998). Hargreaves (2005) described the purpose of feedback as to inspire, motivate and cause the learner to think and most importantly to promote deeper learning and understanding.

- *The development of an argument* – Using the literature to develop a coherent argument.

This extract is the opening paragraph of the literature review. Parveen argues that because assessment has such high stakes within the current climate, it is vital that assessments are both valid and reliable and that they are used formatively to inform practice.

No area of education policy is as contentious – or as consistently newsworthy – as assessment (Mansell and James, 2009). Rightly or wrongly assessments have become the bedrock of educational accountability; they are the predominant means by which students themselves gauge their competency (Sadler, 2007), with summative assessment data also providing parents with key information when it comes to school selection (GTCE, 2011). As much as educationalists may scorn the power attributed to summative assessments, how many parents would perceive a school unable to achieve consistently good 5 A*–Cs as a suitable place for their child? Indeed, schools unable to achieve an acceptable level of A*–C grades are being placed under threat of closure (Assessment Reform Group, 1999). It is undeniable that assessment – a blanket term which should in all fairness refer to a myriad of methods used to collect data (Black & Wiliam, 1998) but is often used meaning summative assessment or tests (Watkins 2003) – has enormous power. As such, we – meaning students, teachers, parents and the government – should be unequivocal on two points: firstly, that assessment data should be accurate and valid and secondly, that assessment data should be used to inform practice and make effective changes to learners.

- *Criticality* – When discussing literature, a critical approach is adopted by raising questions, highlighting any weaknesses or limitations, by introducing other authors' criticisms and by offering constructive solutions.

The example below demonstrates a number of these processes.

Feedback in the classroom should operate from teacher to pupils and from pupils to teacher (Sadler, 1989). The teacher's role is to communicate appropriate goals to identify how the work can be improved, to model how to get there and to encourage pupils to do this for themselves. However, Torrance (2001) argues that detailed feedback on such a regular basis could actually mean that students become more dependent on the teacher, rather than less as it was originally hoped. Another issue that needs to be raised surrounds the amount of time taken in providing detailed verbal or written feedback. One solution might be to include more opportunities for peer assessment.

Thinking it through

If you can, when you have completed your literature review, engage in some peer assessment of a partner's work by highlighting the use of these different strategies with different coloured highlighter pens.

Can you identify any which are underused or overused?

Have you used any strategies that you haven't found here?

Is there a successful balance between references to literature and the student's own 'voice'?

Drawing it together

In this chapter I have outlined strategies for developing a critical approach for engaging with literature to support your inquiry. I have focused on writing a substantial literature review, but it is important to reiterate that this is not the only place in an account of an inquiry where you will refer to the literature you have read. You will need to do this throughout, particularly when analysing your findings and when outlining your conclusions in order to demonstrate that you can make links between theory and practice.

References

Assessment Reform Group (1999) *Assessment for Learning: Beyond the Black Box*. Cambridge: Cambridge University School of Education.

Assessment Reform Group (2002) *Assessment for Learning: 10 Principles*. Available at http://www.assessment-reform-group.org/publications.html (Accessed: 23-Aug-11)

Bell, J. (2005) *How to do your Research Project*. Buckingham: OUP.

BERA (2011) *Ethics in the Educational Research Context*. Available at http://www.bera.ac.uk/ethics-and-educational-research-2/#ethics (Accessed 31-Aug-11).

Black, P., and Wiliam, D. (1998) *Inside the Black Box*. London: Kings College.

Clarke, S. (2001) *Unlocking Formative Assessment.* London: Hodder & Stoughton.

Dann, R. (2002) *Promoting Assessment as Learning: Improving the Learning Process.* London: Routledge Falmer.

Denby, N., Butroyd, R., Swift, H., Price, J. and Glazzard, J. (2008) *Master's Level Study in Education: A Guide to Success.* Maidenhead: Open University Press.

DfES (2004) *Pedagogy and Practice: Teaching and Learning in Secondary School. Unit 19 Learning Styles.* Norwich: HMSO.

General Teaching Council for England (2011) *Key Stage 2 Testing and Accountability Review Response from the GTCE* 2011, London: GTCE. Available at http://www.gtce.org.uk/documents/publicationpdfs/dfe_ks2testing0211.pdf (Accessed: 23-Aug-11).

Gipps, C. (1999) Socio-cultural aspects of assessment. *Review of Research in Education*, Vol. 24, pp. 355–92.

Gipps, C. Hargreaves, McCallum, B. (2000*) What Makes a Good Primary Teacher? Expert Classroom Strategies.* London: Routledge.

Gove, M. (2011) *The Moral Purpose of School Reform.* Available at: http://www.education.gov.uk/inthenews/speeches/a0077859/the-moral-purpose-of-school-reformscale%20study (Accessed: 23-Aug-11).

Hargreaves, E. (2005) Assessment for learning? Thinking outside the (black) box. *Cambridge Journal of Education*, Vol. 35, No. 2, pp. 213–24.

Mansell, W., James, M. and the Assessment Reform Group (2009) *Assessment in schools. Fit for purpose? A Commentary by the Teaching and Learning Research Programme.* London: Economic and Social Research Council, Teaching and Learning Research Programme.

Moon, J. (2008) *Critical Thinking.* Abingdon: Routledge.

Poulson, L. and Wallace, M. (2004) *Learning how to Read Critically in Teaching and Learning.* London: Sage.

Sadler, D. (1989) Formative assessment and the design of instructional systems. *Instructional Science,* Vol. 18, No. 2, pp. 119–44.

Sadler, D. (2007) Perils in the meticulous specification of goals and assessment criteria. *Assessment in Education: Principles, Policy and Practice*, Vol. 14, No. 3, pp. 387–92.

Thomas, G. (2009) *How to do your Research Project.* London: Sage.

Torrance, H. (2001) Assessment in education: Principles, policies and practice. *Education*, Vol. 14, No. 3, pp. 281–94.

Watkins, C. (2003) *Learning: A Sense-Makers Guide.* London: Institute of Learning.

Research on Teaching: How Teachers Can Use Data to Reflect on their Practice

Louise Tracey and Matt Homer

Chapter Outline

Introduction

So you've decided on an inquiry question. You are now wondering how on earth you are going to find an answer. At this point in your inquiry, you may perhaps feel like you're at a complicated intersection in an unfamiliar city with roads leading everywhere. You are finding that one of the challenges of inquiring in the classroom is that there are many different ways in which the answers can be sought; and methods matter. The methods you choose will influence what you find and how robust those findings are. So think of this chapter as a sort of navigation aid. This chapter will help you to determine the most appropriate inquiry methods for your chosen topic, as well as help you decide how to approach the generation, analysis and presentation of the data. In addition, it will help you to critically appraise your inquiry and also incidentally the approaches that others have taken in similar inquiries.

We start by looking at why evidence is important, then go on to introduce two important concepts before discussing some ways of generating data for your inquiry. Next we consider how to analyse and present your data before ending the chapter with two case studies.

Why evidence is important

Ultimately an inquiry is only as good as the data or evidence upon which it is built: evidence has the power to challenge or support what we believe. Research and experience show that evidence and belief have a circular relationship: social constructivist theory actually tells us that we analyse and interpret new data based on our past experiences and beliefs (James Wertsch, 1997). As teachers, we all have ideas about what works or what we believe should work in the classroom. Yet our beliefs are there to be challenged and it is important to question those fundamentally held ideas and ask, 'What is the evidence?' The more effective teacher often has the clearer idea of why she or he is choosing a particular course of action and although the link between evidence and practice is not always straightforward, our convictions are the stronger and our actions more certain when we are convinced about the evidence base for what we do. After all, if a doctor proposed a new treatment we would want it to have been properly researched before it was prescribed and given the vast amount of research in education, it seems naive not to challenge our existing beliefs: they may even be confirmed!

Two important distinctions

Validity and reliability

It's obviously helpful to have some idea of how 'good' a research method is. In reality we can't know this precisely but we have two measures that can give us a sort of guide.

The first is *validity,* which is a measure of how well an inquiry method gives us a picture of the truth. For instance, an interview where somebody is being completely honest is more valid that one in which the interviewee lies. Of course, the complication, which you've probably spotted, is that we don't always know when people are telling the truth. In reality, you need to use your judgement about validity. Questionnaires given out by a headteacher to her staff asking for names at the top might have questionable validity because what staff then write might not accord with what they really think. Gathering evidence in a highly structured way like through the use of multiple choice questions might similarly be challenged on grounds of validity as respondents won't necessarily find an answer they agree with. So you should bear validity in mind as you inquire or read the work of others. The key question to ask is, 'how far is my evidence being affected by the way I am gathering it?'

When we refer to an inquiry as *reliable,* it means that you can be confident that similar conclusions would be reached if it were to be repeated at another time, either by yourself or someone else. Think about classroom observation here. When you watch a lesson, what you're seeing might be typical or it might be unusual. What happens in a lesson might be influenced by the time of day or the lesson that preceded it or by particular children being absent or by many other factors, all of these potentially affect the reliability of your evidence. If you repeat a classroom observation, even if it's the same class or pupil you will find an observation schedule helpful in achieving consistency. Of course, you might also wonder if your presence in the room is affecting what you see but that is a question of validity! Generally, you improve reliability by repeating, by using a larger sample or by standardizing what you do; for example, by using a script of questions when you interview somebody.

Validity and reliability are two helpful conceptions to bear in mind as you carry out your inquiry or read the work of others. Understanding and applying them will help make your evidence more convincing as well as making you a more critical reader of research.

Quantitative and qualitative

Another pair of terms you'll come across are *quantitative,* which refers to data in the form of numbers, and *qualitative,* which describes verbal, visual or other non-numeric data. The distinction is helpful because by and large the two sorts of data are treated differently although the notions of validity and reliability apply to both. You'll see that we refer to the two types of evidence in places later in this chapter but for now the main thing to bear in mind is that your inquiry can involve generating, analysis and presenting either or both of these sorts of data.

We now move on to address a question commonly asked by those starting out on inquiries.

How many is enough?

The question of how much evidence to collect is always a difficult one, particularly for those new to research. However, it is not merely the number of people you choose to talk to, survey or observe that is important, but also whom you pick that is absolutely key to the quality of the findings.

In qualitative studies, the inquirer has to use her judgement to decide, for example, how many interviews is enough to ensure some level of reliability. Of course, there is a limit to the amount of time you can spend collecting data, and also importantly, analysing data. For an in-depth case study a single subject might well be enough. However, care should be taken wherever possible to try to make the sample at least carry some representativeness, hence it might be better to have fewer subjects that are more 'representative' of the population as a whole than opt for as many interviewees as possible. So, for a study based on secondary school teachers' views on classroom management you might consider including a representative range of subject-specialist teachers or a balanced gender profile of interviewees.

In quantitative research, the issues are quite different, and the whole philosophy behind selecting a sample is based on the idea that those in the sample are 'representative' of the population as a whole. If, for example, you are a maths teacher and you use a survey to ask colleagues about particular aspects of pedagogy then your findings are likely to be different if you ask only your maths colleagues rather than a range of subject specialists. The key issue here is one of inference: what are you trying to find out and to whom does it apply? If you are interested only in the pedagogic approach of maths teachers then obviously asking maths colleagues is fine, but if you are trying to answer a broader question about pedagogy more generally then you need to ensure that your sample is drawn widely from the teacher population, and not just based on, say, teachers you know.

In your inquiries the ability to use a random sample and large sample size is likely to be more limited than in an academic research study carried out by full-time researchers. However, there's no reason why you can't include large-scale elements as part of your inquiry. For example, you might complement an inquiry into English attainment in your school with an analysis of English results from publicly available league table data. Don't forget either, that it's perfectly acceptable to try to replicate the findings of a larger research study on a smaller scale. Your inquiry does not have to be entirely novel and it will often be stronger if you borrow from published research.

Thinking it through

Choose a piece of research related to your area of inquiry. Discuss how the sample size contributes to the study. What do you know and think about the composition of the sample and the sample selection? Would you have changed this in any way?

Think about the parallels between validity and reliability that we have discussed here and the same question in relation to assessing pupils. For example, multiple choice questions are sometimes considered to sacrifice validity for reliability. Can you think why this is said? What forms of assessment would you say were particularly valid and which particularly reliable?

Data generation methods: Observation, interviews, surveys

Your inquiry question may be answered by already existing data, be it a national dataset (e.g., Key Stage 2 results) or something specific to your classroom (e.g., Year 9 artwork). However, the chances are that you will have to generate your own data to aid your research. Common methods of generating data which you will have come across and have maybe undertaken yourself at some point in the past are through observation, interviews and surveys.

Each of these methods has advantages and disadvantages and it is important to be aware of them when you are designing your inquiry. How do you match your question to a method? How can you best answer your inquiry question? Can you use more than one method? Would this enrich your approach or complicate it given time constraints? You should always remember, however, that the method is the tool by which you are seeking information and should not be the driver of the information you gather.

As we said above, when choosing a method by which to generate your data you might like to consider what research has already been done in this area. It may be that you have read or seen a technique you would like to replicate to assess whether the results are applicable to your own situation.

Once you have chosen your method of data generation you will need to design your *research instruments*, be they an interview schedule (a list of questions to ask), a questionnaire or a grid for recording observations. We have previously referred to 'qualitative' and 'quantitative' techniques but the methodologies themselves are not so clear-cut. Interviews and observation are often categorized as qualitative and questionnaires as quantitative methods. However, observation can involve counting the number of times a particular habit or practice happens in the classroom (quantitative) as well as exploring the interactions between teacher and pupil in a particular lesson (qualitative). Likewise, an interview can produce numerical data, such as the number of times pupils mention 'praise' or 'shouting', but it can also provide explanations and understandings of a phenomena: for example, why pupils feel praise as opposed to shouting is a positive teacher behaviour.

Below we detail some of the issues you may wish to consider when designing your inquiry (although the list is not exhaustive):

- Do I want to ask open or closed questions? Does the respondent have a list of responses to choose from or can they give a unique answer?
- Am I interested in attitudes? If you are, then a Likert scale (a five-point scale of strongly disagree, disagree, neither agree nor disagree, agree and strongly agree) in a questionnaire or a 'feeling' question in an interview may be appropriate.
- Am I interested in facts? If so, you'll need to choose a method that allows you to track, for example, the number of times a specific event occurs in a classroom, or say the amount of time teachers spend out of school planning and preparing lessons
- How may I be influencing the validity and reliability of my results? As an observer am I affecting what occurs in the classroom and how can I minimize that effect? Do my questions lead interviewees or respondents to a particular answer? Am I unduly biasing my inquiry?
- How long will it take for my respondents to answer all these questions? Are they all necessary?
- Does my observation/interview schedule or questionnaire focus on the research question? It can be easy to become distracted, especially when observing or interviewing.

- How will I analyse and present these findings? We will discuss this further below but it is important to start to think about analysis and presentation *before* data generation begins, not after. For example, when interviewing you may feel that in order to compare experiences it may be particularly useful to have an interview schedule and to ask the same questions of different subjects. Alternatively if you wish to have a case study approach you may choose to have a quite unstructured interview and follow the lead of the person you are interviewing.

The above gives only a very brief overview of the things you should consider when choosing a research method and designing your inquiry. As we've said before, you can explore your ideas further using the current literature in the area you are researching. For example, many researchers include their questionnaires, interview and observation schedules as appendices in their published reports or are happy to share them on request. You could choose to use these as a starting point for your own inquiry design. The research methods texts recommended at the end of this chapter will also be useful when designing your methodology. It can be useful to ask your colleagues to review your research instruments or, if possible, pilot them on someone who would not be part of your inquiry sample. Importantly, however, whatever approach you chose you should keep a record of the decisions you have made along the way so when you are reporting on your data you can be clear about the validity and reliability of your approach.

Thinking it through

In what ways could the methodologies detailed above be used to answer your inquiry question?

What methodology have you chosen to use? Why? What are the advantages of this approach? What other methodologies did you consider?

What are the disadvantages of this approach? How might you address these?

Case studies

A further way of exploring your inquiry topic is through developing a case study or case studies. Each case study is an in-depth analysis of a particular unit or organization be it a school, a classroom or an individual student. It also tends to have a longitudinal element: it studies or reflects on a specific period of time, for example, the way a classroom changes over the period of a term, or a pupil's school career since starting in education. The subject of the case study can be chosen either because it is a typical case and the nature of the in-depth analysis enables us to explore a circumstance in more detail in order to better understand and generalize or it can be unique, and therefore help us to understand the way in which a particular set of circumstances have produced a result we are trying to understand better.

The use of video as a research tool

Video is often used as a form of professional development. It is a useful tool, for example, in observing the way in which we interact in the classroom. Similarly it can be a powerful method of generating data for your inquiry topic. It can also be a useful resource when interviewing subjects as their body language and mannerisms can be captured in a way not accessible by voice recorder alone or can be used as a starting point for discussion, for example, in a focus group. When using video, however, you must, as with any research, be clear about the uses to which you are going to put it, how you will analyse your data and how you will present it. As with other research methods, ethical issues and participants' right to anonymity are also important. You might also consider using video to gather *secondary* data. An example of what we mean by this is: 1) you video a piece of classroom action and then 2) watch that action with a pupil or pupils using the video as a prompt. 'What were you thinking here?' 'Do you understand what you are supposed to be doing here?' The data you generate here isn't the video itself but rather the recording of the interview. You could, naturally use the same approach with colleagues rather than pupils. The value of this approach is that the video is a very effective interview prompt and can illustrate interactions between people that are very difficult to describe in words or discuss in the abstract: watching a piece of video together can spark some interesting ideas as well as being an effective form of professional development in itself.

Analysing and presenting qualitative data

Deciding the methods used for your research can be very important, but just as important is deciding how you are going to use the data and as we have said, this should be taken into consideration at the initial research design stage. When considering how to analyse your data you need to be sure of the questions you are going to ask of it. For example, when designing your interview schedule you will have focused on specific topics if you had a structured interview; a semi-structured interview would have allowed the interviewee to have more of a participatory role in determining the content of the interview; whereas a completely unstructured interview would effectively have been lead by the interviewee. How, then, do you decide to make sense of the data?

You could decide to take the responses to each question in turn and categorize or 'code' them. This will then give you quantitative data on how many interviewees responded in a particular way but also (hopefully) qualitative data as to why they did so. However, that approach may mean that you miss references to the same area mentioned later (or earlier) in the interview that may have been taken into account to provide a fuller analysis. That might, or might not be fine, depending on the research question. However, the opposite approach, to do a *grounded analysis* based on what respondents say, with little regard for the questions asked, might mean you lose your focus on the central inquiry questions you were originally interested in, but it may also provide you with ideas which you had not considered previously. As always, the approach is determined by the research question, not vice versa. And it is important to remember that the 'unusual' case can be as instructive as the 'norm' provided you can explain why it is pertinent within your research question and explore further.

Analysing and presenting quantitative data

Statistical analysis of quantitative data should always be driven by the research questions motivating the research. As with qualitative data above, you should have some idea of what you are going to do with your data when you design your research instruments rather than post hoc 'data mining' 'on the off chance'. Once data has been collected, it may be helpful to put it into electronic form if it isn't already as might be the case in an online survey, for example, by using an internet tool such as SurveyMonkey (www.surveymonkey.com). Any process of data entry might lead to transcription errors and so once data entry is complete some rechecking against hard copy is good practice.

There are a number of useful packages that can aid your analysis including EXCEL and SPSS. Whichever package you chose, however, the initial stages of analysis should include getting to know your data.

- How many cases do you have? How does the sample breakdown by key subgroups?
- Does anything look wrong or surprising (perhaps because of data entry errors or mistakes in coding)?
- What do the responses to particular questions look like?
- With Likert scale responses (see above), are all respondents tending to agree with all your questions? In other words are the responses heavily skewed to one end of your scale? This might call into question your initial survey questions and affect the suitability of certain more sophisticated analyses.

Graphical methods are always very useful. A single graph, well-drawn, can tell you so much more than a table of figures, and you are more likely to gain proper insights from visual representations of your data, even from very simple approaches (e.g., bar charts, scatter graphs, box plots).

Once an initial exploration has been carried out, then it makes sense to focus on the main research questions that the data is intended to address. There are any number of statistical tests that can be employed, but they each bring their own assumptions and require specific types of data to be used appropriately. Again, graphical presentation of, say, sub-group differences, provide more understanding than does a table of figures. Prior to undertaking any research, and in conjunction with designing any research instruments you should determine the type of analysis suitable for the questions you are asking. For further information on statistical analysis we would recommend Field (2009) and Pallant (2010).

What follows are two case studies that utilized different methodological approaches in order to answer the inquiry question asked; one using quantitative data and one qualitative data.

Case study: Peer tutoring — a quantitative analysis

The inquiry question

Simon was a primary school teacher working with a Year 5 class in a single-form entry school. He had been concerned about his class's standard of maths since they had moved up from Year 4 and he was concerned that they would not be prepared for either the Key Stage 2 SATs the following year or to move onto secondary school. He had been focusing on maths during the first term but was still not seeing the type of improvement he would have liked. He started researching methods of improving mathematics attainment and came across an article describing a peer tutoring scheme.

The research described had evaluated a form of tutoring in maths which involved co-operative learning, pairing students up to work together in teams. It also involved pairing students by ability – one high ability; one struggling in maths – to help each other. The evaluation was in the form of a randomized control trial: that is half the schools involved implemented the scheme and the other half carried on with their normal mathematics teaching. When all the children in both groups were assessed before and after the scheme was implemented, those who had been peer tutoring clearly made the most gains in attainment.

Simon decided to research peer tutoring further and discovered that there were different arrangements, including a cross-age peer tutoring scheme which also seemed to produce good results but he felt that, given the logistics in the school, and that he felt it was only his own class who were not meeting expectations in this subject that peer tutoring would perhaps work best for him. So Simon decided that he would introduce a peer tutoring scheme in maths in his own classroom starting from the next half term.

The methodology

Simon was already in the practice of assessing all the children in his classroom for maths and Literacy each half term. He continued to do this as normal. He then implemented a peer tutoring scheme in maths which involved pairing children up in mixed ability teams for one maths lesson every week. He was very clear to the class about how the maths lessons would be changing, how they were expected to behave during cross-peer tutoring time and what he expected they would get out of the new system. He sometimes found it hard to implement the approach as had not seen others do so but kept a checklist of things he should ensure happened every time this method was implemented. In this way he tried to ensure that the method was introduced with fidelity. Apart from this he assessed the children at the end of the half term as usual.

Simon chose to conduct two types of analysis. First, he compared the gains in attainment of his students over the half term during which he had introduced peer tutoring in maths with those in the half term previously. Second, he compared the attainment gains during the same half term with those of his Year 5 class in the previous year. In the former analysis he found bigger gains than when he had used his usual maths teaching methods. In the latter analysis he found that his class were not at the same level as his year group had been at this point in time the previous year but they had gained more from their initial starting point. All this filled Simon with hope for their future mathematics achievement. In addition, Simon felt that the class had improved in other areas as a result of peer tutoring, including in their social-emotional development and interactions with their peers although he did not have evidence to prove this.

Presenting the data

Simon wrote a paper for his masters course which detailed his original classroom dilemma, followed by the reading he did surrounding peer tutoring and the findings from those studies. He detailed how he applied the research to his own situation and the decisions he made while doing so. He graphed the results from his students showing their gains over the half term and compared them with his Year 5 class the previous year. The results looked good but he also explained in which ways they did not replicate the original research he had read; because he found it difficult to implement peer tutoring on his own but he also explained the ways in which he felt that he could move the project forward in his classroom in the future and, importantly, his criteria for evaluating the project's success or failure.

Thinking it through

Critique Simon's methodology – what would you have done the same? What would you have done differently? And why?

Simon used already existing sources of data for his research? Are there any other sources he could have used? Do you think he could/should have generated additional data of his own? Why do you think that?

If you were Simon, what steps would you have taken to disseminate your data?

Where would you take the research next?

Case study: Cross-age tutoring — a qualitative analysis

The inquiry question

Sarah was Head of Year 8 in a large 11–16 secondary school. There had been concerns about the interactions between year groups, challenging behaviour and the social-emotional development of pupils across the whole school. Sarah had heard of a scheme called cross-age tutoring which involved reorganizing the whole school's tutor groups scheme to include pupils of all ages in any single group. The literature Sarah had read suggested that this helped pupils in their interactions with their peers and those of different age groups, helped bring the school together as pupils were no longer banded by age group when it came to tutor groups and challenging behaviour was reduced. It was also suggested that it was a good precedent for preparing students for life after school: in particular, helping them to adapt to the workplace where there was a range of age groups. However, Sarah could not find any evaluations of the scheme that satisfied her or evidence that the scheme did as it said. Having said that, she was intrigued by its claims and thought it may be a solution to some of the concerns that had been expressed within her school.

The methodology

Sarah decided to speak to some of her colleagues about her ideas. In particular she felt it was important to speak to other year heads as the implementation of such a scheme would affect their work directly, and she felt they would be most informed about the social and emotional well-being of their students (as well as their receptiveness to a new scheme). Consequently she conducted 30-minute interviews with the heads of Year 7, Year 9 and Year 11. At the beginning of each interview she described the cross-age tutor group scheme as she had heard it being implemented in other schools. She allowed her interviews to be fairly open because she did not have any other research on the subject to follow but also because she wanted to allow the year group heads to provide some ideas of their own. She did, however, have some areas which she knew she would like to be addressed so her interviews were semi-structured and she asked specific, open-ended questions about their initial reactions to the idea of such a scheme; what areas of the current tutoring system they felt could be improved; and what, if any, concerns they would have about a cross-age tutoring system being implemented within the school.

Sarah transcribed all three interviews and then started to form a coding scheme by which she could make sense of the answers the year heads had given her. In addition to the answers to the specific questions she had asked, Sarah looked for recurrent themes throughout the interviews and any contradictions in what the year heads had said. She also thought about the structure of the school and its current composition and how that may affect a cross-peer tutor group scheme.

Sarah's next step was to approach two schools who had implemented a cross-age tutor group scheme and interview two year heads within each school about the process of implementing such a scheme, what they felt the benefits and drawbacks were and finally, she detailed the concerns her own year heads had described and asked them how they would address or had addressed them. Again, the interviews were semi-structured and Sarah transcribed and coded them. She used the same coding frame but ensured that she was able to tell the difference between the schools using cross-peer tutor groups and her own school who was only considering it.

Presenting the data

Sarah used her interview data to address the issues surrounding the implementation of a cross-age tutor group scheme within her school. She presented it as part of a masters assignment but she stressed that the data she was presenting was more about the views of the heads of year at the two schools than the actual consequences of such a scheme. Having said that, Sarah was able to directly correlate some of the concerns the teachers at her own school expressed with solutions, or at least, the ways in which the schools implementing the scheme addressed them. Overall, Sarah felt quite positive about what she had seen and that the scheme could be applied to the situation in her own school.

To this end Sarah presented her findings in a staff meeting towards the end of the school year. The teachers in her school were, however, concerned about the extent of upheaval that would be caused by such a change and didn't feel that there was sufficient evidence to justify it. They did, however, agree with Sarah that there was a need for change, particularly in the area of interactions between different year groups. Sarah suggested implementing a mentoring scheme within the school whereby older year group members mentor students lower down the school. The teachers agreed to try this.

Thinking it through

Do you feel Sarah answered her research question? Why, or why not? How, if at all, would you have done things differently?

Why do you feel that the teachers agreed to implement the cross-peer mentoring scheme as opposed to the cross-age tutor group scheme? How might Sarah have better presented her evidence? What evidence would you want to see in order to implement either scheme?

What do you think Sarah should do next?

Drawing it together

Research can sometimes seem to be a big, imposing, field. We have covered what our experience tells us are the most important questions you need to address when thinking about how to inquire. To explore these issues in greater depth, we would recommend Derek Rowntree (2000), Louis Cohen et al. (2007) and David Hopkins (2008) as reference sources. We would stress that it is important above all that you should approach any written research with a questioning attitude (what? why? who? when?). This is the same attitude with which you would approach your students' work so why not approach research in the same way? Other people's research can help and inform your own practice. We are not suggesting that you should apply every new practice or idea to your own teaching but rather consider what the evidence is and how it applies to your own situation. As important, however, is how do we generate and reflect on our own teaching data in order to improve our own practice and the life chances of our students? We hope that this chapter has helped you to understand not only the ways in which you can do this but also the importance of doing so.

References

Cohen, L., Manion, L. and Morrison, K. (2007) *Research Methods in Education (6th Edition).* Oxford: Routledge.

Field, A. (2009) *Discovering Statistics Using SPSS (Introducing Statistical Methods series) (3rd Edition).* London: Sage.

Hopkins, D. (2008) *A Teacher's Guide to Classroom Research (4th Edition).* Buckingham: Open University Press.

Pallant, J. (2010) *SPSS Survival Manual: A Step by Step Guide to Data Analysis Using SPSS (4th Edition).* Buckingham: Open University Press.

Rowntree, D. (2000) *Statistics Without Tears*. London:Penguin.

Tymms, P. et al. (2011) Improving attainment across a whole district: school reform through peer tutoring in a randomized controlled trial. *School Effectiveness and Improvement*. Vol. 22, No. 3, pp. 265–89.

Wertsch, J. (1997) *Vygotsky and the Social Formation of the Mind*. Cambridge: Harvard University Press.

Research in Teaching: How to Harness Everyday Teaching Activities as Teacher Inquiry Methods

Fiona Woodhouse

Chapter Outline

Introduction

Why should teachers inquire in their classroom? As teachers we are aware that we should ensure that pupils know why we ask them to do a particular task, partly to encourage them to engage with the task and partly to produce better outcomes. The same is just as true for us as teachers; we need to have a clear understanding why we should inquire in our classroom. Once we are clear on the why, the next question is the how. In Chapter 2 you can read about research methods at a macro level and you will be introduced to some of the key ideas and techniques you will need to deploy in gathering evidence for your inquiry. In this chapter I am going to focus much more on the micro level of inquiring, helping you to translate what you have learnt into your own classroom and your own practice. I am going to introduce you to some techniques and skills that will help you to inquire while you are teaching, probably on a full time table.

Thinking it through

What do you feel are the biggest challenges faced by teachers wanting to undertake classroom inquiry as part of their normal practice?

How could the school help to militate against some of these and support inquiry?

Can you identify someone on the senior management in charge of CPD? How could they help to support inquiry within practice? What might you do to facilitate this?

Inquiry: The practical considerations

There are lots of books that can help you to identify research tools and methods to use in the classroom; Chapter 2 in this book gives an overview and this chapter will carry additional examples of research methods, but there are few books that help a teacher on a full timetable to see ways in which they can find the time and the resources to be able to even contemplate the thought of undertaking an inquiry. The purpose of my chapter is to try and tackle these issues and offer some ways in which the daunting could become the achievable.

Let us begin with the most obvious challenge for any teacher: time. Schools are busy places, whatever the popular belief. I have never yet met a teacher whose day begins at nine and ends at three with no work in the holidays! How can we find time in this hectic and pressured profession to take on more work in the form of classroom inquiry? Hopefully in chapter one we have made a powerful case for the moral imperative that underpins inquiry, better teaching and therefore better learning for children with all that that implies, but it still can feel like a huge mountain to climb. So how can we make time for it?

1. Inquiring is a normal part of teaching, not something different. You can, and should fit your inquiry into your normal planning, teaching and assessing of pupils. Lessons need to be planned: as teachers you are always tweaking and reviewing and reflecting. Inquiry only formalizes this process. For example, imagine you want to meet the needs of a pupil new to a reception class in a primary school who has a hearing impairment. This pupil has to be planned for

in any event: conducting an inquiry can help you to focus on the provision you need to put in place for the pupil and can equally help to evaluate the effectiveness of that provision.

2. Data can (and often should) be collected in lessons. It is not always something that has to be done outside the lesson at lunchtime or in the evenings. I am going to explore specific methods of data collection later in the chapter but much of the data that matters to you arises out of the lesson; pupil work, lesson plans, resources you use are all forms of data that can be analysed. The lesson itself can be recorded. If you want to know how pupils talk to each other when they are trying to work co-operatively to solve complex maths problems, pop a recording device on their desk and record them (mobile phones can be great for this, they are so ubiquitous now that they are invisible and therefore pupils forget they are being recorded). Observing while you are teaching is challenging but still possible; observing what pupils are doing can be as simple as keeping a tally of boys/girls hands up or as complex as recording the physical movement of a pupil in the room. You do not always have to be the observer either, teaching assistants, a colleague, a video camera can all be fantastic observers of what we do (you can read more about the use of video in Chapter 2).

3. Work with colleagues. This is something this book has tried to facilitate in every chapter because it has been shown to work. Teaching should be about sharing practice and inquiry is a great way to do this. Divide some reading between you and a colleague and summarize it for each other; share data collection on the same question; take it in turns to observe each other. Be a critical friend if you are writing up for masters level. Schools often don't feel like places where adult learning is valued: working with colleagues using an inquiry approach is one way to highlight how important adult learning is in making better teachers.

The second hurdle to inquiry is often resources. Professional researchers have opportunities to bid for funding for their research; for teachers this is next to impossible so how can resourcing be supported?

1. Use your local universities. If you are a student on an M level programme you will have access to the huge advantage that is a university library. It is slightly odd that the place where most research about teaching in schools is held is outside those schools but this is a product of history and cost: journal subscriptions are very expensive. As an M level student you can also use the ICT facilities including software licenses to data coding programmes like Nvivo, MAXQDA or SPSS. If you are not on a formal masters programme, do you have trainee teachers in your school from a university programme? If so, then it may be possible to have guest access to the library. If neither of these is an option, sign up for the Department for Education research bulletin, read your union magazines or follow your subject association's publications and updates. All of these provide excellent stimuli for inquiry.

2. Pool resources. Does your school library have any books on teaching and learning? If not consider asking if some can be bought for staff to share; there are excellent books on special education needs, on assessment and so on, that would be of benefit to all staff and could be a really cost effective use of the CPD budget.
3. Don't be put off because you work with very young children or children with additional needs. Not all data that you collect has to be written; ethical considerations apply but then they do to all children so don't be put off, be creative (see point 4 for an example).
4. Use everyday technology. Professional recording equipment would be fantastic but even for full time researchers is not usually possible. Mobile phones, tablet computers, domestic digital cameras, webcams and even plain A4 paper and a pack of crayons should all be seen as easily available resources you can use to collect data. You are collecting data that is of use to you, which will tell you something; it doesn't have to be fancy or full of technical wizardry to achieve that. Asking a four year old to draw what they love about the classroom is as deep and insightful a piece of data collection as any videoed interview.

These are the two most frequently cited reasons for being worried about undertaking inquiry but I think there is a third that is just as common: confidence. It might have been a very long time since you were engaged in 'academia', or indeed it might be all too dreadfully recent; both can make you feel that this is something that other people do not you.

1. Perfection is not an option. This is as true of the most academic large scale research as it is of your classroom inquiry. Things go wrong; if you could go back you would do it differently. The fire alarm will go off. You will forget to turn on the recording equipment. The child you are doing a case study on will vanish to the Canaries for two weeks at an inconvenient moment. Accept this, acknowledge the possible effect it may had had on your findings and move on. It happens to all of us and it is OK.
2. It will make you a better teacher; I promise!

Using research methods in the classroom

Having explored some of the barriers to inquiry and hopefully made them seen smaller, the rest of this chapter explores several types of data collection methods that have been used in classroom and in other educational settings to gather data to explore research questions. The methods are grouped to explore how different students have used the methods as part of their own successful research.

Case study: Exploring pupil engagement with the curriculum

Louise is a science teacher in her third year of teaching. She is just beginning to be familiar with the science curriculum but does need to teach science topics outside of her own discipline. She wanted to look at a strategy of working with a local initiative of bringing a current researcher in science into her classroom. With this new teaching strategy it was hoped that her pupils would be more engaged in a difficult subject (Physics). So Louise wished to see whether this strategy would have any impact on their performance. Time was an issue, so Louise began by giving her pupils a questionnaire at the beginning of one lesson to take an initial snapshot into their present engagement with the subject. She then repeated the questionnaire at the end to try and ascertain if there had been any changes to their perspectives and engagement. This gave her some data but she decided to add more and one lunchtime brought together a small discussion group (focus group) to explore what the outcome of the questionnaires had suggested and whether there were other issues that had arising from undertaking this research. This also helped to triangulate and ensure reliability of the data she collected from the questionnaires. Additionally, she compared modular tests results from the previous physics module and the second physics one taken after using the new teaching strategy to see if there had been any changes in their performance. She also used national published data and school data from other classes to help with this analysis. So in order to explore her initial question Louise used the following research methods.

- Questionnaire
- Focus group interviews
- School data and other published data

These methods will be described below.

Questionnaires

These are a very popular way of collecting data quickly. The design and use of questionnaires is an area that you will find much written about to help inform your own design (see Louis Cohen et al., 2011, Bill Gillham, 2008, and Pamela Munn and Eric Drever, 2004). The questionnaire can collect a range of data both quantitative and qualitative, it can be administered to a large number of respondents, it is often easy to analyse and can be done without the presence of the researcher. Some of the issues with using questionnaires are the limited response rates, the poor quality responses to some of the questions and the time taken to construct, pilot and modify the questionnaire.

When choosing questionnaire as a research method, there are several different things that need to be carefully considered. What aspect of the research question are you seeking to address? It is important to be clear for whom the questionnaire is designed and what sort of information you are seeking to generate. Who the questionnaire is intended for is important in choosing the language, layout and length of the questionnaire. Shorter questionnaires with shorter answers may be more useful in the classroom with young pupils. The literacy levels of intended respondents also need to be considered in terms of the vocabulary used or whether alternatives to words should be employed: for example, do you need to use smiley faces to frowning faces instead of words? Do you need someone to read the questions and record the answer for some pupils? How is the questionnaire to be administered? Will it be sent by post or put in pigeon holes, carried out by telephone or e-mail, or through an online means such as SurveyMonkey (www.surveymonkey.com) or even by texting. Would you be present to clarify and ensure the return of the questionnaires or will they be filled in by participants alone?

Once these decisions have been clarified you then need to think more carefully about the questions that you to ask and any additional information that will help you analyse the data (age, sex, gender, etc.). There are several forms of questions that can be used.

- *Closed questions* are where there is a range of or prescribed responses that can be given: these can be particularly useful for quantitative analysis.
- You could use *dichotomous questions* which require a yes/no response and will often be used to direct the respondent to the appropriate next question, for example: if you answered yes go to . . .
- You could have *ranked response* questions: a series of statements which the respondent has to rank in order from 1 to 10.
- There are *multiple choice* questions where a range of answers are given and the respondent has to 'tick all that apply'. A popular rating scale is the Likert scale where there is a range of responses (strongly agree, agree, neither agree nor disagree, disagree, strongly disagree).
- A *semantic differential scale* gives two opposing adjectives with a scale between for the respondents to select an appropriate response between the two adjectives (e.g., like 1 2 3 4 5 6 7 dislike).
- *Open type* questions can give more information but does need to be piloted to ensure they are clear and unambiguous. These open-ended questions will give

space for the respondent to answer a question that has some guidance into what the questionnaire is wanting or may begin with a question stem that the respondent continues to answer.

Once you have drafted your questions, you need to carefully go through and check that you have sequenced your questions in the correct order, that you do not lead respondents towards particular answers or introduce any other sort of bias in the questions. Finally, it is always time well spent if you can pilot the questionnaire to see if it works. By this, I mean anything from giving it to a similar group (say a class other than the one with which you're going to use it for real) to showing it to your partner one evening. The more people see it before it's used; the more chance that ambiguities and other problems are seen. By this stage you will have difficulty seeing these glitches: you will simply be too close to it.

The final process in using a questionnaire is the analysis of the data generated. Have sufficient returns been received to ensure that the data is valid? Have the questions been correctly answered to begin the analysis of the data? As you can read in Chapter 2, there are a number of techniques you can use to analyse what you have be it quantitative or qualitative data.

Focus groups

These are another popular and useful way of collecting data and are part of the data collection tools in education. They involve bringing together a small group to discuss the issue in which you are interested. You can readily see how this might be done as part of a lesson: for example, you might have a discussion with a group of students on peer assessment or what they find easy or difficult about a subject or how they feel they learn best. David Morgan (1997) explores the use of focus groups in more detail. Often they are used in education to *triangulate* findings from other data collection mechanisms.

Triangulation simply means using more than one data generation method to look at the same thing: for example, you might have a question, say about learning styles in a questionnaire and then probe the same area in an interview. Doing this means that you can bolster the validity and particularly the reliability of your data as a repeated response intuitively carries more weight. You can read more about triangulation in the book by Louis Cohen et al. (2007).

Care should be taken on selecting the members of the focus group. Too many and it is difficult to get the group to discuss things in detail. As I'm sure you can imagine, it is particularly difficult to get numbers of children to settle on a particular topic in depth. On the other hand if your focus group is too small, you may not get a broad range of views. Again consideration as to the members of the group needs to be given: they all need to be able to contribute without one or more dominant characters discouraging others from participating or being able to contribute. This is particularly important when putting pupils into focus groups.

Careful thought also needs to be given on how to lead the discussion. Usually this is in the form of some leading questions or statements that the group discuss. Most focus group activities are voice or video recorded with the researcher additionally making notes to supplement and clarify the information.

All of the above points illustrate factors that could potentially undermine the validity of evidence derived from focus groups and of which you should therefore be aware. Nevertheless, I would encourage you to use focus groups, particularly with pupils as they are easy to fit in to your normal work pattern. Provided you ensure that pupils are clear that the focus group is a place where they can express their feelings without judgement and in which they are not expected to give 'right' answers, they can offer a responsive way of accessing pupil voice in a way that can be less channelled and limited by you as an inquirer. The chances of the truly unexpected viewpoint turning up in a focus group is perhaps greater than in any other means of inquiry and for that reason you should certainly consider their use.

School and national data

While you will probably need to generate data of your own for your inquiry, there is a large body of existing evidence available for you to access in the form of school data. The school of today is a data-rich place and the following is by no means an exhaustive list of the sort of evidence that you might use:

- Fisher Family trust (FFT) and/or Jesson band data
- data from published school league tables
- statistical analysis by departments/ year groups; for example, reading ages or National Curriculum levels
- the register of special needs
- attendance data
- socio-economic data such as numbers of pupils on free school meals
- data on gender and ethnicity
- behaviour log data
- attendance at parents' evening
- numbers of pupil participating in school clubs

There will also be data that local authorities publish on their websites which will allow you to compare your school data with other schools in your region. There is also a wealth of national data available from the Department for Education Statistical Gateway (www.education.gov.uk/rsgateway/), the National Foundation for Education Research (www.nfer.ac.uk) and Ofsted (www.ofsted.gov.uk). You should also consider the subject associations as there may be data available there which could be useful. Finally, published research reports are another source of data and they also give you an insight into the methods used by researchers which you may well be able to adapt for your own purposes.

Case study: A reflection on developing peer assessment within the classroom

Beth is a teacher with 20 years' experience who has a Teaching and Learning Responsibility (TLR) for literacy. She was asked to develop a strategy for integrating peer assessment into Key Stage 2. Beth wanted to ensure that this was done correctly and she had good evidence to support her when she had to develop this with the whole staff in Key Stage 2. Beth initially spent some time researching into peer assessment, looking at what it is and how to use it. She then began to adapt some of the strategies she had read about but she wanted to evaluate how effective then were with the class before incorporating them into her teaching across all the groups. She understandably wanted to know herself what the evidence suggested about the effectiveness of this approach before committing to something of which neither her nor her students had much experience.

To evaluate her intervention as she went along, Beth kept a journal in which she jotted down any observations she had about how she felt pupils were reacting to the peer assessment activities she initiated. Beth augmented this evidence by interviewing selected pupils during the term as she began to embed peer assessment more comprehensively in her teaching. The research tools Beth used and which are described below are:

- Interviews
- Journals.

Interviews

These are a popular research tool for the collection of data. Steinar Kvale (1996) provides an excellent discussion of the range of different interviews and how they can be used to elicit information. The key characteristic of the interview is that it gives an opportunity to exchange information, both verbal and non-verbal, and allows the researcher to question responses and gain a richer layer of information. Equally, a well-conducted interview gives the respondent the chance to clarify questions or raise their own points. In an ideal interview, neither party should leave wondering, 'I wonder why that was never discussed?'

In most standard texts you will read that interviews may be categorized according to how structured they are. I'm not sure that this is a helpful distinction for classroom inquiry. I think it very unlikely that you will ever interview a participant using a structured interview approach: which you might think of as a sort of 'call centre script' where the questioner dare not diverge from the rubric. Structuring interviews is a means of improving their reliability and making sure that the inquiry themes are addressed particularly when you have a team of interviewers and neither are pressing issues for the sort of small-scale inquiry you will be involved with.

It will be far more important in my view that you think carefully about the *validity* of your interviews. How will you assure the person you interview that nothing they say will be passed on to a third party? How will you make sure your questions do not dominate the interview and exert unnecessary influence on what your interviewee says? Both of these particularly, but not exclusively, apply to interviews with children. How will you put your interviewee at ease and get them to open up?

In answer to the first question, openness is a good strategy; allow your participant to suggest questions before you meet, ensure that you clearly say that you will respect their anonymity, offer them a transcript of the interview. The best strategy to address questions 2 and 3 is courtesy. Allow the first question to be a chance for them to 'get things off their chest'; something like, 'So how are things?' is all you need.

Making notes during an interview is difficult and hampers you in thinking of follow-up questions so it's always best to record the interview: mobile phones are an excellent way of doing this as they are so unobtrusive and flexible. Remember to tell your interviewee that you are doing so. You also need to take into account aspects such as the location of the interview: a 'neutral' venue such as an interview room in a school will avoid the 'Headmaster's study' syndrome!

As mentioned above, interviews are usually recorded and transcribed. However, recently Jean McNiff and Jack Whitehead (2011) have discussed research that is being presented with media files both audio and video. These can provide direct evidence of what has been said in interviews and actions that have been undertaken and observed including expressions and body language. You might want to consider the paper by Michael McMahon (2010) on enhancing motivation of pupils to learn using a virtual learning environment, which includes audio files as well as similar papers on the website http://ejolt.net/.

Diaries, journals and logs

Not all research methods need be complex. Simply keeping a diary, journal or log, call it what you will, is a highly recommended method for helping you to think through your project as well as acting as a source of data in itself. When you are teaching or working flat-out you will find that you can have great insights into your inquiry and there is a danger that these, often priceless, ephemeral thoughts will be lost unless you make a note then and there. The mobile, smart phone, tablet or laptop, or even an exercise book, can be a great organizer of your thoughts. Record these scraps of thought as they happen and they will coalesce and build into bigger ideas and concepts. Also don't forget the potential for thinking aloud into a microphone when you have a moment: you may have your greatest ideas when cooking!

Your diary entries will probably consist of descriptions of what has happened together with some form of reflection on your own action perhaps with a commentary of your own learning from this or further action points that you might need to address. Donald Schön (1983) describes two main forms of reflection: 'reflection in action' and 'reflection on action'. *Reflection in action* is when you need to reflect on what is happening and make practical decisions about the next form of action, often very quickly as in a classroom situation, whereas *reflection on action* occurs later and at a more relaxed pace when you have been able to look back on what happened, process and reflect on the decisions made and the learning that you have gained from this.

Additional research tools

There are additional research tools that you can use beyond those that Louise and Beth have employed. In an assignment from a head of department who wanted to consider the use of technology with his Year 11 science class including emails for handing in homework and the use of wikis in class Stuart used an online survey and email evidence as his research tools.

Online surveys

These include web-based surveys and emails with attachments to web links and are proving to be an increasingly useful tool for data collection. Questionnaires can be complex and time-consuming to produce yourself but there are now many templates and online surveys that you can use. You simply add in your questions and for some of these, small numbers of questionnaires can be prepared and administered free of charge; a common one in many education areas is the SurveyMonkey website, referred to earlier, while an alternative may be found at http://free-online-surveys.co.uk/.

These products are relatively easy to use and may often collate the data for you. However, as with questionnaires that are paper based, careful thought needs to be given both to the compilation of the questions and the layout of these surveys. Don Dillman (2007) has given a useful overview of using online surveys as a research tool to collect data. Louis Cohen et al. (2007) have given an excellent commentary on the use of online surveys including a review of the problems and possible solutions. They also present what research suggests as effective practice in the use of online surveys. One of the areas that they do stress is that you should keep the questions simple and try and avoid open-ended questions that can be interpreted in many divergent ways. Online surveys can be particularly useful methods for surveying pupils who will often respond to web based activities more readily; however, care needs to be taken from an ethical perspective as the confidentiality of your data may not be guaranteed.

Another important method that can be used to collect data from the classroom is observing lessons. In looking at using the teaching strategy of assessing pupil progress (APP) in a science lesson, Rebecca used observation to record how pupils engage with an APP task in using the prompt sheets she had devised. Rebecca combined her own observation with those of a classroom support assistant who was based with her during the lesson; however, it could easily have been another teacher who had time to quietly observe the activity.

Alternatively, as mentioned earlier, she could have asked someone to video the lesson to support her with the data collection.

Observations

Observations of events, lessons and so on, are useful ways of gathering data. Observing is a skill of watching and listening closely to the incident and then analysing what has been observed. An advantage of observations is that

> [they] are not dependent on the respondents' own views or interpretations of the research questions but rather rely on gathering evidence though the eyes and ears of the researcher. (Castle, 2010, 69)

Observation will allow you to observe the activity in situ and to record critical events as they happen. This method does not require any investment of time from the people being the focus of the research. The value of observation, however, rests on interpretation of the events observed and two people might see the same action and come away with different notes of their observation (we might question the reliability of the observation if this is the case).

As with so many things in life, the value of observation is greatly enhanced by good preparation. First, assuming that gaining permission to observe is not an issue, you will need to think clearly about exactly what you are going to observe, how this fits in with your inquiry questions and how you are going to record your observations (you can read more about this in Chapter 2 and in Louis Cohen et al. 2011). Next, you need to decide the extent to which you will take part in what you are observing. Non-participant observation may feel more artificial to you and to other teachers and pupils, although lesson observation is a much more common feature of school life now than it was in the past. The big advantages of non-participation are that you minimize the effect of being there and you leave both hands free, as it were, to record what you see. To many teachers, participant observation, in which you take part in what is going on, feels more natural, and you may end up doing this even if you start out hoping not to participate when, for example, a child comes up to you and asks you to do something! Naturally, you use both forms of observation in the same lesson or session, drifting in and out of taking part and this is perhaps the most natural way for you to observe a classroom, especially in your own school.

Participant observation is, of course, what you can do when you are teaching your own class so in terms of convenience; this is the preferred way to observe. The weaknesses, as I'm sure you'll appreciate, are the difficulty of physically recording what happens and on a practical level it can be hard actually to see beyond what you are immediately engaged with: the pupil with whom you are working, the book you are looking at. In a more profound sense, it is difficult to disengage and see things afresh: when you are constantly working in your familiar 'teacher' mindset, it is hard to adopt the 'inquirer' role, but that's a general issue you will face in all forms of classroom inquiry.

It is good practice in terms of the validity of your observation to be able to discuss those observations with participants to help ensure that your interpretation of events is similar to theirs. Of course, there may be sound reasons why your interpretations diverge significantly, but this conversation will still help you confirm that you saw what you thought you saw.

Rebecca also used the work completed by her pupils as data for her research study which is a very useful source for understanding many of the questions we need to ask ourselves about the classrooms in which we work.

Pupils' work

This is a useful area to consider when collecting and presenting evidence and, of course, the pupils' work you collect can take many forms. It can be copies of work completed by the pupils in their books, whether photocopies, scans or photos (again smartphones are excellent for this). It could be posters or presentations that children have made.

Often, and particularly with younger children, it is difficult to get pupils to complete questionnaires or articulate what they are feeling, so the use of alternative ways need to be found. Children could use smiling faces to mirror how they feel, drawing pictures which they then can explain later when you interview and record what they say. Rebecca in her research used copies of the activities pupils had produced.

Jayne wanted to understand what pupils understood about the characteristics of a good teacher. Her secondary pupils completed a free essay with very little guidance, simply being given the initial phrase 'a good teacher . . .' This was a small sample of 30 pupils and her data was therefore in the form of a textual analysis, an analysis which explored words and common phrases between all the pupils. With some primary pupils, Jayne asked them to draw a teacher, and their pictures were discussed with the children on an individual basis to unpick what they had drawn and why. This study indicates that you can employ several different ways of collecting the data depending on the group selected but still focus on the same research question.

Pupils as researchers

As a classroom teacher, you can always get the pupils to collect the data for you. Bob wanted to look at activity during lunchtime around the school but felt that if he were to go round it would affect what was happening too much. So he got a small group of students to take cameras out during lunchtime and asked them to take photographs of what they saw around the school. This provided a rich source of data. The students were not directed in any particularly area; neither did Bob share with them the whole research question that he had formed. Other studies have seen pupils to give out and analyse questionnaires as part of their own lessons, which have then been used directly for the teacher's own research. One of the most interesting outcomes from this is how the pupils often enjoy and feel valued to be part of the research process. It is surprising that so few texts seem to recommend the use of pupils as researchers given the potential contribution that their participation could make to your inquiries and to their own education. There are, as Priscilla Alderson and Virginia Morrow (2011) write, caveats about involving pupils in this way in certain sensitive areas, especially where they might be asked to comment on each other or on members of staff, but your own sense of professionalism will no doubt alert you when there are ethical doubts like this. In Chapter 7 you can read a case study involving pupils as researchers.

The theme of this chapter, however, has been how to combine inquiring with full-time work as a teacher, and involving pupils as co-researchers can be one of the most economical ways to do so.

Thinking it through

Having now read through these forms of data collection and seen how other teachers have used them for their own research, what methods would be appropriate for the collection of data for your own teacher inquiry?

Drawing it together

This chapter has considered the ways that you as teacher in your classroom can employ research tools as part of your own teaching to ask questions and develop your own practice. Research is a powerful tool and it has been a privilege for me to watch how teachers, when they begin to ask questions and seek evidence to help answer these questions become more reflective teachers.

It has become apparent to me that through engaging in inquiry, teachers have developed their relationship with their pupils as well their confidence in taking risks in their own teaching to enable better learning, the outcomes often going beyond the original question posed. I will end with this quote from Beth's master's thesis, which indicates this quite clearly.

> . . . but perhaps on a personal note, one of the most enjoyable parts of this study has been the positive impact on my relationship with a group of Year 9 students, who are pleased with the impact this study has had on their grades. (Beth: unpublished master's thesis 2011)

References

Alderson, P. and Morrow, V. (2011) *The Ethics of Research with Children and Young People: A Practical Handbook*. London: Sage.

Castle, K. (2010) *Study Skills for your Masters in Teaching and Learning*. Exeter: Learning Matters.

Cohen, L., Manion, L. and Morrison, K. (2011) *Research Methods in Education*. Oxford: Routledge.

Dillman, D.A. (2007) *Mail and Internet Surveys: The Tailored Design Method(2nd edition)*. New York. John Wiley & Sons.

Gillham, B. (2008) *Developing a Questionnaire (Real World Research)*. London. Continuum International Publishing Group Ltd.

Kvale, S. (1996) *Interviews: An Introduction to Qualitative Research Interviewing*. London: Sage.

McMahon, M. (2010) How do I enhance motivation to learn and higher order cognition among students of science through the use of a virtual learning environment? *Educational Journal of living Theories*. Vol. 3, No. 2, pp. 170–92.

McNiff, J. and Whitehead, J. (2011) *All you need to know about Action Research(2nd edition)*. London: Sage.

Morgan D.L. (1997) *Focus Groups as Qualitative Research(2nd edition)*. London: Sage.

Munn, P. and Drever, E. (2004) *Using Questionnaires in Small-Scale Research: A Beginner's Guide*. Glasgow: Scottish Centre for Research in Education.

Schön, D. (1983) *The Reflective Practitioner: How Professionals Think in Action*. New York: Basic Books.

Part 2
Inquiring into the Mechanics of Teaching and Learning

Inquiring into Teaching, Learning and Assessment

4

Claire E. Smith and Barbara Hibbert

Chapter Outline

Introduction

Regardless of location in the world, the fundamental business of any classroom teacher is:

   (i) to *design activities* to ensure that his/her students learn;

  (ii) to *teach* to aid *progression in understanding*; and

 (iii) to *assess* the progress of those learners across a period of time (e.g., across a year, or a Key Stage, or an examination level and so on) usually in a particular area of subject expertise (i.e., within the curricula subjects timetabled in any one learning environment).

Such processes are so accepted as part of the essence of what it means to teach that it can be tricky for expert teachers to deconstruct why it is we teach in the manner we do. This chapter considers some of the roots of teaching, learning and assessment, from both official and theoretical perspectives, as well as giving the inquiring teacher some suggested approaches into researching various processes of teaching and learning.

What is good teaching and learning?

At a time when UK government influence on the curriculum is seemingly ever shifting, it can be difficult for the teacher at any Key Stage or age phase to see beyond requirements for the latest policy initiatives, for example, personal learning and thinking skills (PLTS), personalization of learning, espoused Ofsted best models of subject practice. Changes in government can herald yet more 'new' approaches to teaching and learning, which sometimes appear diametrically opposite to what was being done in the classroom before an election, and to what was listed to be periodically inspected. Fortunately, in Western education, some fairly constant underpinning themes for the processes of teaching and learning have endured into the early twenty-first century behind such whims and trends.

A diligent teacher should first establish for themselves a definition of what it means to *teach* and to *learn*. Learning is a highly complex aspect of human society, present from pre-historic existence onwards. However, the constant issue for teachers in modern-day classrooms is that learning can be more or less effective, and that it appears to manifest itself differently according to the peculiarities of a class in front of the professional on any given day. The professional teacher's developmental role should be to understand the processes at work in learning as well as possible in order to teach so as to benefit their students' learning. One of the characteristics of effective teachers is their ability to understand the many processes at work in a classroom of learners so that educational philosophies and polices that come along at various times in a teacher's career (such as the most recent Ofsted focus on students' learning rather than teachers' teaching) can be placed into a wider educational context of learning theory, knowledge and application.

There are numerous learning theories that have developed since public education became compulsory in the late nineteenth and early twentieth centuries in the Western world. Most teachers are somewhat familiar from their own initial training of specific theories for learning, such as:

- Bloom's Taxonomy of lower to higher order skills (from knowledge, to comprehension, to application, to analysis and to synthesis and evaluation) (Bloom et al., 1956)

- Kolb's four-stage Active Cycle of Learning (concrete experience (CE) – doing/ experiencing something → reflective observation (RO) – reviewing/reflecting on the experience → abstract conceptualization (AC) – concluding and learning from the experience → active experimentation (AE) – planning and trying out what you have learnt). Kolb argues also that this cycle of learning can be attached to four distinct learning styles: Diverging (CE/RO); Assimilating (AC/RO); Converging (AC/AE); and Accommodating (CE/AE) (Kolb, 1983)
- Various VAK approaches to learning (i.e., visual, auditory, kinaesthetic learning approaches) which have largely morphed out of Howard Gardner's Multiple Intelligences work (i.e., linguistic, logical-mathematical intelligence, musical intelligence, bodily-kinaesthetic intelligence, spatial intelligence, interpersonal intelligence, intrapersonal intelligence) (Gardner, 1993)

In various ways, educational jurisdictions across the Western world have incorporated aspects of the above theories of learning into their 'learning systems' in the hope that learners at whatever stage or age improve in their understanding and perform better in assessment situations. But the root of much of our curriculum learning and assessment approach comes from two main traditions of learning theory – that of behaviourism and constructivism. Each represents very different types of learning experience for a learner. Elements of each can be seen at work within all subjects currently being taught in the National Curriculum.

In a solely 'behaviourist' classroom, learning is assumed to come from the external environment acting on the students' ability to learn or understand. Students are therefore passive, they learn only as individuals, and they are extrinsically motivated to learn (by some kind of reward, such as a GCSE grade). The job of the teacher is to transmit the relevant knowledge and skills necessary for such success. If you were to look at a classroom based on behaviourist traditions, you would notice the students listening to a teacher for a lot of the time, students would individually work on an exercise/s to reaffirm the taught knowledge, and all learning would follow a logical, linear expectation of whatever the subject discipline requires.

Conversely, in a purely 'constructivist' classroom, learning is assumed to occur through interaction in the social context between students, and between teacher and students. Essentially, it is what is commonly known as 'active' learning in today's classrooms, where students are intrinsically motivated (they want to learn from within themselves, not for extrinsic reward). The constructivist teacher's role is to provide opportunities to construct knowledge and skills gradually through learnt experience, so that her learners will build up their own sense of what the subject is, rather than inflicting an externally and already defined idea of what it is. If you were to look at a classroom based on constructivist traditions, you would notice the students making, experimenting, playing and acting. The individual student would choose his approach to learning about the theme under investigation, and the direct experience of 'playing' with that theme would allow the learner to explore it in his own way and at his own pace.

Of course these are polar extremes for a learning environment and most classrooms in schools today combine traits from each of these learning traditions to form what the school and/or the subject ethos deems the better way to learn. As a practising teacher, it is easy to choose a preferred approach to learning that sits more in one tradition and then simply dismiss the other. But without exploring the roots of each approach further than their simplistic traits, a teacher is unlikely to see how each can benefit the learning, teaching and assessment processes to full effect in her context.

Behaviourism as a theory of learning was espoused in particular by B. F. Skinner (1904–90) and Edward Thorndyke (1874–1949), both working in the early to mid twentieth century when objective, scientific rigour and observable stimulus dominated research in educational psychology. At this time within research, scientific rigour was preserved because researchers used only observable behaviour as data. Any internal 'mental' states of learners were hypothesized from behavioural traits observed to explain phenomena. Observable stimuli were always 'external', and behaviours were then associated with particular conditions created by those stimuli. In Skinner's case the experimentation was often done on animals to condition learning responses.

Therefore, according to Skinner (1974), all teachers needed to learn was how to teach, the 'how' being deduced from observable learning behaviour. Thus teachers 'need only to be taught more effective ways of teaching' under certain conditions. While this approach for learning sounds relatively simple, objective and individualistic, several of Skinner's tenets bear reflection and considerable relevance for our twenty-first-century classrooms. For example, Skinner believed that:

- positive reinforcement was more effective at changing/establishing behaviour than punishment.
- five main obstacles to learning existed for learners:
  (i) a fear of failure;
  (ii) tasks were not broken down into small enough steps;
  (iii) a lack of direction affected successful learning;

(iv) a lack of clarity in directions affected successful learning;

(v) a lack of positive reinforcement affected successful learning.

- any age-appropriate skill could be taught using *five principles to remedy* the above problems. The teacher should:

  (i) give learners immediate feedback;

  (ii) break down any task into small steps;

  (iii) repeat directions as many times as possible;

  (iv) work from the simplest to the most complex tasks; and

  (v) always give positive reinforcement.

Few twenty-first-century teachers would reject such ideas, and even fewer would state that these do not feature in more successful classroom teaching environments.

Likewise, Edward Thorndike's behaviourist learning theory had several underpinning principles which few teachers ignore in a twenty-first century classroom. Thorndike (2010) suggested that for human beings the most basic form of learning has always been by trial and error. He stated that learning is incremental rather than insightful – so our learners do not necessarily have light bulb moments without essential pre-scaffolding from prior learning. He suggested that learning is not mediated by ideas but by experiencing something in action and in reality. Thorndike therefore devised certain laws attached to such learning, which present useful ideas for today's classrooms:

- Law of *readiness* – according to Thorndike, a learner has to be ready to learn or perform something. Any interference with goal directed behaviour causes the learner frustration. Equally, making someone do something they do not want to do is utterly frustrating. When a learner is ready to perform some act to do so proves to be a satisfying experience. When a learner is ready to perform some act, and then cannot do so, it becomes an annoying learning experience. When a learner is not ready to perform some act and then is forced to do so, it is a vexing experience.
- Law of *exercise* – according to Thorndike, humans learn by doing. We forget by not doing (think about the modern languages or the mathematical equations you learnt at school and can hardly recall because you have not used them regularly since school). So connections between a stimulus and a response are strengthened as and when they are used (he called this the law of *use*), Conversely, connections between a stimulus and a response are weakened if they are not regularly used (law of *disuse*).
- Law of *effect* – according to Thorndike, if the response in a connection is followed by a satisfying feeling or experience, then the strength of the connection is considerably increased. Conversely, if the response to a learning experience is followed by a sense of frustration or annoyance, then the strength of the

connection is marginally decreased. So if a learner in a KS3 classroom enjoys her lesson, and her learning, and understands what it is the teacher set out for her to learn, she is far more likely to transfer that learning to future lessons than if the learning experience has been negative and unsatisfactory for her.

Thorndike also noted that humans will normally try multiple responses to solve a problem before it is actually solved. Consequently, one shot at learning and performing something is not usually going to be enough for most learners to be able to really understand what is possible. Equally, he recognized that what knowledge the learner already possesses in the moment of the learning experience influences a learner's behaviour while learning a new task. Thus a student's prior learning experiences or the present state of the learner affects the possibilities for his learning. He called this the learner's *set* or *attitude*. The latter point is critical for the twenty-first century classroom – how the learner solves a new problem is affected by the solution techniques he has to solve problems, which are analogous to previous challenges he has faced. Whatever stimuli the teacher places in front of the learner will therefore potentially echo the response a learner associates with another type of stimuli (Thorndike called this *associative shifting*).

If so many tenets of behaviourism seem relevant to the twenty-first century classroom why don't all educators solely advocate that approach in their classrooms? In essence, from the early to mid twentieth century another field of educational thinking known as *constructivism* developed. In many ways, constructivism extends and builds on the work of behaviourism. However, there is a major difference between the ways the two learning theories developed. Whereas behaviourism centred on observable external behaviour, constructivism was, and still is, a serious study of *'mental' functioning* (i.e., what is going on inside a learner's mind) that calls on multiple disciplines to tackle this unknown world of the mind (anthropology, linguistics, philosophy, developmental psychology, computer science, neuro-science, psychology). Equally, in constructivist learning theory the *situated nature of learning* is deemed as influential and important (e.g., in studies of Jean Lave and Etienne Wenger (1991), and Kenneth Rogoff (1991) where the impact of social/cultural influences on the context of learning are explored).

A particularly famous early proponent of more constructivist ideas was Lev Vygotsky (1896–1934) who worked at around the same time as the behaviourists Skinner and Thorndike. Vygotsky (1978) believed that the active role of learners with others who play a role in supporting their learning was critical.

Alongside such social interactivity, the role of the social environment including tools, cultural objects and people, was essential in developing human thinking. He is particularly renowned for his *Zone of Proximal Development* (ZPD) which he defined as the distance between the actual developmental level as determined by independent problem solving and the level of potential development as determined through problem solving under adult guidance or in collaboration with more capable peers. According to Vygotsky, then, what learners can do with the assistance of others is *even more indicative* of their mental ability and potential development than what they are able to undertake alone. This does, however, imply that the learner wants to learn and is ready to do so with help, and can be pushed to the upper level of their potential competence at any one time. Nevertheless, a learner's potential will always be changing as the learner grows in independence over time and masters certain concepts, principles or approaches pertinent to a subject – in other words the 'buds' of development become the 'fruits' with growing competence. An easy way to remember Vygotsky's ZPD concept is that a learner's *actual* developmental level is always retrospective (looking back at what they have already learnt and can do independently) whereas the mental development possible with peer or adult help and guidance will always be prospective (looking at what it is possible to understand in a learner's mind once taught). For twenty-first-century classroom practitioners concerned with progression in students' understanding, this is critical research.

A later constructivist whose work as a psychologist has been particularly influential in terms of understanding human cognition and the way in which culture guides and influences our educational systems is Jerome Bruner (b. 1915). Bruner (1960, 1966, 1986) suggested that learners should always know the structure of the disciplines they learn so that they become active problem solvers and not just assimilators of information from those disciplines. In other words, with the correct conceptual tool box, a student can make sense of the world they live in, in their own way. He recognized that there were three ordered ways that learners transform experience into knowledge:

(i) through action;
(ii) through imagery;
(iii) through a range of symbolic systems around them.

Education was therefore a negotiation and a conflict between these three modes of representation as learners internalize the tools that generations of humans have constructed over hundreds of years. It was such cultural psychology (i.e., the historical background and current forces of a culture) which was a critical force for learning. Therefore for Bruner, education was not just the function of a school, but a function of the culture-at-large that a learner was learning within. Our students construct knowledge in the cultural milieu of their context and in collective environments both inside and outside of school. Active agency within this milieu exists in any human being, and a collective conviction about the constructions of human knowledge is inculcated from an early age. Bruner was concerned with the purpose, the goals and the means in learning stating clearly that 'intellectual activity is anywhere and everywhere, whether at the frontier of knowledge or in a third grade classroom' (Bruner, 1960, 14).

Thinking it through

How much impact have theories such as constructivism and behaviourism had upon your classroom practice?

Can you identify aspects of whole school policies that appear to have been influenced by one or other of these theories?

Both behaviourism and constructivism offer much for our classroom practice, and for studying learning that occurs in any setting. However, each also attracts their critics. Criticisms of behaviourism (Anne Jordan et al., 2008) suggest that learners may not connect to understanding (except superficially); that behaviourist approaches make it difficult to motivate all learners in class all the time; and that as a theory behaviourism ignores the major demand of differentiation, and is therefore more likely to create passive learning environments. Criticisms of constructivism suggest that to be adopted fully and embraced properly would require huge logistical implications (time, resources, etc.); that constructivism assumes all students are motivated and responsibly autonomous for their learning; and that both of these characteristics would tend to lead to a classroom where management issues often dominate for the teacher/educator.

You can read more about research into learning from the National Research Council (2000) and Sue Dymocke and Jennifer Harrison (2008).

> ## Thinking it through
>
> Consider how learners learn in your context:
>
> Is learning about the construction of knowledge for the individual or does learning occur because learners interact with others?
>
> What does learning in your setting depend on? Genes, your school, socio-economic background, culture?
>
> Kyriacou (1997) writes that teachers should not always teach children to their preferred learning style.
>
> Why do you think he suggests this? Is he right?
>
> How do you define the purpose/s of learning?
>
> How do you define the purpose/s of teaching?

What is good assessment?

Of course there is a third and looming dimension to learning and teaching in school settings across the world also – that of assessment and its place within the learning and teaching systems all educators teach within.

> Education is always, in a sense, about the tension between 'what is' and 'what might be'. The role of the teacher is to support learners in moving forward to higher and higher levels of attainment. (Pollard (ed.), 2010)

It may seem unarguable that the purpose of teaching is that students should make progress. Nevertheless the last two decades in the UK have seen an ideological battleground focused firstly on what constitutes progress and how such progress can be measured. The battle has also focused on the use of formative and summative assessment, and which is more appropriate in which circumstances. A third issue has been how consistency of measurement of progress within and across institutions can be achieved. Some practitioners claim that too much assessment has negative effects, that measurement does not lead to growth, as in the old Russian proverb, where too much time spent weighing the pig means that fattening it is forgotten. Conversely, some school management teams seem to believe that progress is linear and constant and demand that evidence of such progress is recorded centrally, as frequently as on a fortnightly basis, and made available to parents for regular inspection.

In England, the formal tools to measure educational progression are National Curriculum Attainment Levels at Key Stage 1, 2 and 3 and GCSE/AS/A level grades at Key Stages 4 and 5. National Curriculum Attainment Target (NCAT) level descriptors were designed and should still be used as a 'best fit' model at the end of the Key Stage and various educational subject communities are vocal in opposing what they see as the abuse of levels by senior managers, some of whom believe it is valid to use NCAT levels on every piece of written work and that learning objectives can and should be levelled in lesson plans. This leads us to consider whether levels can be used in a formative way throughout the Key Stage or whether they are only fit for the purpose of the end of Key Stage summative assessment. Many schools seem to use sub-levels as a tool of measurement, often with three divisions, for example, Level 5a, 5b and 5c, but sometimes even seeing the level divided into ten. GCSE grades are self-evidently summative measures, awarded at the end of a course for work that is completed in controlled conditions, whether in a modular way at the end of each unit or by external examination at the end of the course. This does not, however, preclude the use of GCSE or A level assessment objectives and criteria in a formative method of assessment throughout an exam course. There are serious debates to be had on whether progression means the same thing in all subjects. In some subjects it may be linear, a ladder to be climbed, whereas in others progression is more like a climbing frame, where there can be downs as well as ups before progress is consolidated. For example, in History, students may seem able to understand the concept of causation easily with one set of material, but struggle with the same concept at a later date when presented with material on a different topic which they find more inaccessible, whether because the language is more difficult or because they have less understanding of the context.

Making this comprehensible to the various audiences for assessment is a significant task for educators in schools. Parents and students see assessment as a means of assessing individual progress against national targets and increasingly students ask if they are a 'level 2a or a level 3c', without apparently having any concept of what these labels might mean, other than in terms of where they stand in relation to their classmates. There have been various attempts to rewrite NCAT levels in 'child friendly' language and hand out proformas which tell students what they have to do to achieve the next level and make 'progress'. Many parents are still confused by 'levels', which, for the majority, came into being after they themselves had left school. For the government and its Ofsted inspectorate, assessment is a means of measuring schools against each other and identifying the strongest and weakest as models of good practice or targets for intervention. For senior managers in schools, assessment can be micro-managed to identify strong and weak departments and for purposes of monitoring individual teacher performance. There is ample room for potential teacher research projects on the use of assessment for the various purposes and audiences identified above. Does the assessment regime in a classroom serve the learners best? Or is it for the people most accountable for the results?

It is unlikely that this multi-purpose regime of testing, assessment and reporting on progress will end any time soon. The challenge for teachers therefore is to make such assessment as meaningful as possible within the constraints of the various audiences addressed and the different purposes served. One aim might be for the learner to be at the heart of the process rather than assessment being something which is done to them, or a tick box exercise which enables school managers to fill in another box on their Self Assessment Form or SEF. Increasingly school data tracking systems require half-termly assessments which show students making neat, linear progress of about two 'sub-levels' a year and two whole levels per Key Stage, and as long as individual teachers and departments produce the figures which support this, few questions tend to be asked.

Thinking it through

How is assessment data gathered at your school?

What evidence do you have parental understanding of the assessment measures you use in school?

What do you feel are the strengths and weaknesses of your current system?

Assessment for Learning, as promoted by Paul Black and Dylan Wiliam (1998), sees formative assessment as a learning tool, setting targets for students to close the gap between their present state of understanding and their identified learning goal. The role of the teacher is thus to ensure that the students understand what that learning goal is, and to encourage self-assessment as students progress towards the learning goal.

The danger, as outlined by Oliver Knight (2008), is that if formative assessment is to be criterion-referenced as Black argues, then feedback can become too much related to criterion compliance, and result in procedure-driven approaches, for example, 'the target sheet in the back of their book outlines exactly what students need to do to "move up" one level, sometimes even including the phrases they should use and tiny procedures they should follow related to sub-levels and slices of levels'. Knight sees this as potentially undermining the original intention of the Assessment for Learning 'Black Box' with the danger of 'measurement at the expense of learning', the sort of reductionism which Black sought to avoid. Where use and misuse of AfL is concerned, there is the potential for individual teacher research projects looking at the experience of students in a particular assessment regime.

Thinking it through

Consider how learners are assessed in your context:

How do you define 'progression' in your subject area? In your department? Across your setting?

What is the difference between formative assessment and summative assessment in your setting?

How is that understanding shared between staff and with students?

How often is the progress of your learners summatively measured in your department? In your setting? Given what you have read in this chapter, is the balance right?

Is learner progress always linear and constant? If not, why not, in your subject area? Does this vary by age group?

When and how are NCAT levels and exam board grades used to assess your learners? What is the underlying rationale for such summative assessment?

Does such summative assessment improve your students' progression in your subject area? Is there any way in which it hinders progress?

Who are the audiences for your assessment data? How do you communicate such data meaningfully to the various audiences you have to show it to?

Black and Wiliam (1998) have argued for the last ten years that assessment is a learning tool to help students close a gap between what they currently know and an identified learning goal. Do you agree? In what ways do you think assessment is considered more or less than this in your setting?

Developing a case study: 'How can I enquire into summative assessment processes at my school?'

The following case study investigates the use of home learning in a secondary school department to develop more effective summative assessment at Key Stage 3 in a small rural comprehensive school.

Context of inquiry

Rashid works in the English department and initially identified a problem; 'traditional' short, weekly, home learning tasks were proving to be counterproductive for some students. There were two discrete issues:

(i) for some students other commitments made it difficult to complete tasks on time to a reasonable standard;

(ii) for others, these types of task did not seem to give them the opportunity to reach higher National Curriculum levels.

In both cases this meant that the summative judgements being made might not reflect the true potential of the students. In this case one can see how the connection between learning, teaching and assessment needed sharper scrutiny and closer investigation in order to assure that summative NCAT levelling was accurately undertaken by teachers in the school.

The Inquiry question

Rashid decided to work with staff from across the department to investigate the question: *Can changing home learning impact upon student progress?*

Methodology

The decision was taken at the start of an academic year by the whole department to investigate the *effects* of changing the approach to home learning through two distinct tactics: (a) set less; and (b) expect more. Common, but imaginative tasks were then designed and set across year groups: one task per half-term. Students were given a choice about how to present their work, and could control when they completed the task, increasing their independence as learners. As well as the completed 'product', students were also required to complete an assessment sheet on which they commented on how they completed the task, what they enjoyed/found challenging and so on. These comments were designed to encourage students to actively engage with the task and also provided a focus for staff feedback.

The aims of the project were to investigate the following impacts:

1. Impact on students
   - Does this change in approach increase their engagement with home learning?
   - Does this change in approach lead to higher standards of work?
2. Impact on staff
   - Does this change in approach enable staff to give more constructive and effective feedback?
   - Does this change in approach give more evidence for awarding NCAT levels to students?
3. Impact on parents
   - Do parents have a better understanding of the holistic grades awarded when larger pieces of work are involved?

Simultaneously, relevant literature and research on home learning was investigated. This suggested various positive advantages to home learning, including most relevantly for this study, how home learning enabled students to demonstrate what they know and understand, rather than passively responding to the teacher in class. Negative outcomes were also identified, for example, a potential increase in the social gap between students, with not all having the resources to complete the work satisfactorily.

Next, a strategic decision on data collection was taken. This had several stages:

1. Gather information about home learning practice in other faculties/departments across the school.
2. Set new home learning tasks using new criteria.
3. Monitor the outcome of tasks completed by the students.
4. Collect students' views on the change in approach via questionnaires: in this case study, over 100 KS3 students were asked to complete anonymous questionnaires about the changes to home learning.
5. Collect departmental staff views via questionnaires; all members of the department were surveyed.
6. Collect parental views on the change in approach; all members of department were asked to make informal enquiries at parents' evenings.

The scale of the data collection involved required that all staff in the department would help to gather the data but Rashid would be the primary data analyst. This collected data was therefore a mixture of quantitative and qualitative so the data analysis reflected this.

The table below shows some of the quantitative results of the student survey:

QUESTION	YEAR 7	<BOX?TABLE	YEAR 9
Were the task sheets easy to understand and complete?	Easy = 50% Difficult = 50%	Easy = 60% Difficult = 17%	Easy = 89% Difficult = 4%
How useful was teacher feedback?	Useful/very useful = 65% Not useful = 15%	Useful/very useful = 72% Not useful = 9%	Useful/very useful = 83% Not useful = 4%
Top 3 words (from choice of 10) used to describe experience	Challenging Chore Worrying	Challenging Chore Engaging	Challenging Satisfying Engaging

Qualitative student comments included:

- *Feedback on your last project means you have goals for the next.*
- *They help you get a 'bigger picture' of your work.*
- *I went over things I'd done in class and now I understand it better.*
- *There were no limits on what you could do.*

Presenting the inquiry

The data was then analysed by Rashid and presented in a departmental meeting. The survey showed that students did find the work challenging, but the comments suggested that students had a better understanding of what they had achieved. Staff questionnaires suggested an increased engagement with home learning and some improvement in the quality of work produced. Overall, staff felt they had a better evidence base and were more confident in awarding accurate NCAT levels. The anecdotal evidence collected from parents, though not generalizable or indeed a valid sample, was largely favourable, not least because parents found it easier to become involved in longer projects. However, more formal and systematic questioning of parents was needed, especially about whether they had a better understanding of the NCAT levels awarded to their children.

Rashid concluded that there were some problems with the nature of the data collection, which could have been tied more closely to the objective of summative assessment. However, there were some interesting wider findings. For instance, the data suggested that this kind of homework could be a powerful tool for the development of PLTS as it encourages students to become independent, reflective learners and self-managers. The results and conclusions of the study led to the department changing its practice to better suit the learning needs of the school's students.

Thinking it through

What could a similar study offer to your setting?

What are the advantages and disadvantages of working together as a group of teachers to collect the relevant data?

How could some of these data collection methods be adapted to use with much younger children?

Drawing it together

- Because teachers work in the classroom all the time, it can be difficult to distinguish the expertise and deconstruct the roots of the knowledge that they already hold.
- A good teacher will deconstruct how they understand the act of teaching, learning and assessing from both their own perspective and that of the learners in front of them.
- Such a dialogue will enable professional pedagogy to be debated more often and with more confidence in any setting.
- Underpinning such understanding, an inquiring teacher will read research and inquiry studies (both empirical and theoretical) to inform their teaching, learning and assessment styles, rather than just adopting new 'fads' wholesale without critique.
- Small-scale case-study work can revolutionize practice if well planned and well implemented. Its results can be transformative.
- Data collection and analysis should allow an inquiring teacher to have a positive understanding of, and impact on their classroom work for the benefit of learners.
- The dissemination of what has been discovered in a case study, however small, is important for the audiences the learning, teaching and assessment is aimed at.

References

Black, P. and William, D. (1998) *Inside the Black Box: Raising Standards Through Classroom Assessment.* Phi Kappa Delta. Available at http://www.pdkintl.org/kappan/kbla9810.htm (Accessed 10-Jun-11).

Bloom, B., Engelhart, M., Furst, E., Hill, W. and Krathwohl, D. (1956) *Taxonomy of Educational Objectives: The Classification of Educational Goals. Handbook 1: Cognitive Domain,* London: Longman.

Bruner, J. (1960) *The Process of Education*. Cambridge: Harvard University Press.

Bruner, J. (1966) *Toward a Theory of Instruction*. New York: W.W. Norton.

Bruner, J. (1986) *Actual Minds, Possible Worlds*. Cambridge MA: Harvard University Press.

Daniels, H., Cole, M. and Wertsch, J.V. (eds.) (2007) *The Cambridge Companion to Vygotsky*. Cambridge: Cambridge University Press.

Dymoke, S. and Harrison, J. (eds.) (2008) *Reflective Teaching and Learning*. Sage, London.

Gardner, H. (1993) *Frames of Mind: The Theory of Multiple Intelligences*. New York: Basic Books.

Gardner, H. (1999) *Intelligence Reframed: Multiple Intelligences for the 21st Century*. New York: Basic Books.

Jordan, A., Carlile, O. and Stack, A. (2008) *Approaches to Learning: A Guide for Educators*. Oxford: OUP.

Knight, O. (2008) Create something interesting to show that you have learned something': Building and assessing learner autonomy within the Key Stage 3 history classroom. *Teaching History*, Vol. 131, pp. 17–22.

Kolb, D.A. (1983) *Experiential Learning: Experience as the Source of Learning and Development*. New Jersey: Financial Times/Prentice Hall.

Kyriacou, C. (1997) *Effective Teaching in Schools – Theory and Practice*. Cheltenham: Nelson Thornes.

Lave, J. and Wenger, E. (1991) *Situated Learning: Legitimate Peripheral Participation (Learning in Doing: Social, Cognitive and Computational Perspectives)*. Cambridge: Cambridge University Press.

National Research Council (2000) *How People Learn – Brain, Mind, Experience and School*. Washington DC: National Academy Press.

Philpott, J. (2010) Assessment, in Davies. I (Ed.) (2010) *Debates in History Teaching*. London: Routledge.

Pollard, A. (2010) *Professionalism and Pedagogy: A Contemporary Opportunity. A Commentary by TLRP and GTCE*. London: TLRP. Available at http://www.rtweb.info/content/view/434/123/(Accessed 5-Jun-11).

Rogoff, B. (1991) *Apprenticeship in Thinking: Cognitive Development in Social Context*. Oxford: OUP.

Skinner, B.F. (1974) *About Behaviourism*. London: Jonathan Cape.

Thorndike, E.L. (2010) *The Principles of Teaching Based on Psychology*. Available at http://www.forgottenbooks.org/info/9781440057113 (Accessed 5-Jun-11).

Vygotsky, L.S. (1978) *Mind and Society: The Development of Higher Psychological Processes*. Cambridge MA: Harvard University Press.

Inquiring into Subject Knowledge

Nick Mitchell and Joanne Pearson

Introduction

Subject knowledge is not only of primary importance in any school teaching (Rosie Turner-Bissett, 2001; Robert Guyver and Jon Nichols, 2004), it is a reason why many teachers become and remain teachers and a passion for teaching particular ideas and content continues to motivate those who teach students of all ages. There is abundant evidence (e.g., Ian Richardson 2006, Viv Ellis 2007) that the most effective teachers have strong, confident subject knowledge. This link is recognized in the Professional Standards for Teachers in England and Wales within which subject knowledge forms an important element in both the current and revised standards for teachers due to be implemented from 2012.

But what is subject knowledge? What can educational research and practice tell us about subject knowledge, and how can you explore and develop the subject knowledge of yourself and of your colleagues?

In a seminal paper in 1987, Lee Shulman argued that good teachers don't simply demonstrate knowledge about their subject (content knowledge); they also need two other categories of knowledge in order to teach well. They require some generalized knowledge about the methods and resources they might use in their teaching (curricular knowledge) and they also need specialist knowledge about how to teach their own subject; about how pupils learn best in their subject; about how to make particular content understandable. Shulman called this last category 'Pedagogical Content Knowledge'. He later refined his thinking, breaking 'subject knowledge' down into the following seven categories (Shulman, 1987):

- content knowledge
- general pedagogical knowledge, such as classroom management
- curriculum knowledge
- pedagogical content knowledge
- knowledge of learners
- knowledge of educational contexts
- knowledge of educational ends

Since then, there has been a lively debate in the literature about the adequacy of Shulman's model to describe subject knowledge. The Teacher Development Agency (TDA) published a document in 2007 in which they put forward a view of subject knowledge with four components. As you can see below, the first three of these could have been taken from Shulman but they have also a category to reflect a view that subject knowledge as a broad term also encompasses a set of *attitudes* towards a subject.

- Subject Knowledge: the essential knowledge and understanding needed to teach a subject effectively.
- Pedagogy: subject theory and practice: an understanding of the teaching skills and strategies needed to teach pupils effectively.
- Pupils' development: an understanding of how learning is linked to pupils' development and their background.
- Attitudes: positive attitudes towards pupil learning that underpin subject knowledge, skills and understanding.

There have been several other attempts to unpack the idea of subject knowledge. Peter Lee et al. (1997) described subject knowledge as:

- The content of a subject: for example, historical events, the workings of the kidney, the eight times table; this is termed *substantive knowledge*.

- How the subject works: how to think like a mathematician or a scientist; this is termed *procedural knowledge*.

These then, are just some of the ways in which educationalists have tried to analyse the idea of 'subject knowledge'. As this brief discussion has shown, the concept is not a simple one and unravelling the notion of subject knowledge in this way requires you to consider a number of questions such as the following:

- To what extent is there a common pedagogy between subjects? For example, are English teachers and PE teachers essentially doing the same or very different things?
- Are our values as individual teachers actually a part of our subject knowledge? Do we, for instance, learn to think in certain ways because of the subject we teach?

One way in which you might start to frame your inquiry into subject knowledge is by trying to match your own ideas of subject knowledge to these different theoretical descriptions. Working with theories in this way is one of the best means of understanding them and the thinking that lies behind them.

Thinking it through

- Discuss Shulman's list of the types of knowledge needed by teachers. How helpful do you find it as a way to examine your own knowledge? Do you think anything is missing?
- Can you identify any particular issues within your school department that relate to substantive, procedural or pedagogical subject knowledge? For example, how confident are you/your colleagues about aspects of substantive knowledge?
- How important, in your view, are attitudes towards a subject? Do your attitudes differ from those of your colleagues who teach different subjects? Are there/should there be 'subject cultures' and what effect might these have on pupils' experiences?
- Brainstorm a list of possible areas for inquiry in this content area. Share them with colleagues in your department and beyond. What would they add?

In the two case studies that follow, we will use the substantive and procedural model of subject knowledge to present two contrasting approaches that students might take when undertaking a professional inquiry into their subject knowledge. Firstly we will consider how you might select and approach some of the literature that will help and guide you in this task.

Reading about subject knowledge

One place to begin your reading about subject knowledge is the National Curriculum (curriculum.qcda.gov.uk). It is important at the outset, however, to realize that each subject forms only part of the overall curriculum. As a result, it is helpful to see the whole picture and it is therefore important to begin any reading on subject knowledge with an overview of the National Curriculum before moving to subject specific information.

For examination subjects you might also consider the assessment frameworks that exist; for example, the Ofqual National Qualifications Framework (www. ofqual.gov.uk) or the websites of the various examination boards.

Approaching your reading in this way, beginning with the larger picture before narrowing your focus to the assessment requirements for one particular subject is one way to ensure that you consider the place and purpose of subject study not in isolation but alongside a wider view of the school curriculum.

Having formed an overview of the governmental picture of the place and purpose of subjects within the curriculum, you can now widen your reading to include other sources. These may include:

- subject association websites and journals
- practitioner created websites
- articles in newspapers and journals such as the *Times Educational Supplement*, Education *Guardian* and so on, and possibly the professional journals of the teacher unions
- any published textbooks written for teachers about teaching and learning within particular subjects

These articles and descriptions of practice outside your immediate setting may help to inform your picture of what is happening in the subject, but also stimulate areas of interest or investigation. It is particularly important here to try and examine your own beliefs about subject knowledge and question some things you may take for granted. As we have hinted earlier, subject areas themselves have different views of the place and role of content knowledge in teaching and it's helpful to see things afresh. So, for example, if you are a maths teacher, you might like to read how English teachers view the place of subject knowledge in their teaching.

Thinking it through

- If you are part of a professional development cluster, compare the ways in which the National Curriculum orders for your subject are similar or different. Are there opportunities for a collaborative approach to this inquiry?
- Bring your key readings to a meeting and précis them for your colleague. Use these summaries to help form a discussion about possible inquiry questions.

Framing your question

The next step is to decide what you are going to investigate and put this into the form of an inquiry question describing (and perhaps most importantly *limiting*) what you want to explore in this inquiry. For example, do you want to investigate teacher subject knowledge alone, or the ways in which this might impact upon pupil subject knowledge?

Above all though, your main concern should be to form a question that is manageable in the time you have and so you should bear in mind the general principles of framing inquiry questions that we discussed earlier (in the Introduction).

Thinking it through

Identify the area of subject knowledge that you intend to explore. Talk about why you have made this choice. Are you certain you will be able to restrict your inquiry to just this aspect?

What might be the sort of ethical issues that arise from the inquiry you have proposed? How might you have to show sensitivity?

Consider what you would do if you are not able to answer this inquiry question? How would you make sure you could still find something to write about?

Developing your inquiry

In this chapter we are going to examine two case studies that explore one of the ways of considering subject knowledge: the substantive and the procedural. These case studies only illustrate two broad possibilities: as we have seen, there are many other ways in which you might conceptualize subject knowledge and therefore ways other than the two that follow in which you might structure your research.

Case study: Inquiring into substantive subject knowledge

The context of the inquiry

Sam began a masters in her NQT year. She is now in her second year of teaching and has a Year 5 class at a primary school in the north-west of England.

Sam had previously identified an interest in science within the primary setting as a particular strength of her practice. She would like to extend this further and has talked to her headteacher about her wish to coordinate science across Key Stage 2 at the school in the future. The school has a one form entry and there are currently four classes at Key Stage 2 with six teachers involved in teaching this age range.

The inquiry question

Sam has had informal chats with other teachers in the school and has concluded that not all of her colleagues are confident about teaching science. The teaching of science at secondary school and beyond has recently received a lot of attention in the media and this has also informed Sam's interest in the nature and importance of substantive subject knowledge in the teaching of primary science. After discussions with her colleagues, Sam framed the following question: *How confident are Key Stage 2 teachers about their knowledge and understanding of science and how does this affect their lesson planning?*

Thinking it through

How relevant is a question of this type to your own school? If you are in a secondary school, do you have many non-specialists teaching particular subjects? If you are in a primary school, how does the school manage the professional development of teachers in connection with subject knowledge?

What other potential questions could you identify for this setting? How many might also be relevant in your own practice/setting?

Do you consider this to be a manageable investigation in one school term? What do you see as the risks to successful completion of such an investigation and how might these be managed?

What do you feel are some of the benefits/challenges of this sort of inquiry for you and for the school?

The supporting literature

Sam needed several key pieces of reading in order to undertake the study. She began with government documents to firmly establish the context within which she and others were working when they teach science, but she realized that she needed to think about the issues around subject knowledge at a deeper level. So she looked on the Association for science Education (www.ase.org.uk) and science Learning Centres (www.sciencelearningcentres.org.uk) websites to see if there were any discussions about the challenges of science teaching that she could use to help her to frame some questions around which she could start to shape her inquiry.

Finally, Sam realized that she also wanted to develop her understanding of the academic literature around subject knowledge. She carried out an online literature search and found several articles in specialist academic journals on this topic.

Thinking it through

What do you think are the strengths and limitations of using 'official' literature from governmental bodies to inform your inquiries?

Try carrying out an online literature search, perhaps using Google Scholar or the British Education Index. Perhaps your university tutor might help with some suggestions to get you started on this.

Select two or three articles from academic journals with some relevance to your topic and briefly look at the methodology the researchers have used. How useful is thinking about this for your investigation? How useful is this for your understanding of the literature as a whole? What lessons might you apply to designing your own inquiry?

The methodology

Sam's inquiry question had two distinct parts: i) finding out about teachers' confidence regarding subject knowledge; and ii) exploring their approach to planning and teaching science. Sam's potential sample of teachers was small and she therefore decided to try and use all six teachers within her school as her research participants. She approached her colleagues and asked if they would agree to help her with this inquiry.

Sam used each teacher to complete a questionnaire and she then conducted a short interview with all six colleagues. The questionnaire mostly addressed the first part of Sam's question while the interviews were designed to probe the second part: teachers' approach to planning and teaching. The interviews were short (about ten minutes) because Sam was aware that even a short interview generates a lot of data. The interviews were recorded and then partially transcribed.

Generating the research data

To generate descriptions of science subject knowledge, Sam took ten statements from the National Curriculum attainment targets from Sc2: Life processes and living things; Sc3: Materials and their properties; and Sc4: Physical processes. Her research participants were asked to rate their level of confidence on each separate statement using a Likert scale from 1 to 5 with one indicating very confident and five very unconfident. At the end of Sam's questionnaire there was a writing box in which the six teachers were asked to expand on their perceptions of their own subject knowledge. Sam then used the data from the questionnaires in four ways:

i. She used the numerical (quantitative) data from the ten Likert scale questions to construct a table of mean confidence levels for the three science content areas and presented this as a bar chart.
ii. She transcribed the comments from the text boxes into a Word document that she used as an appendix for the assignment she had been asked to write.
iii. She used both the text box comments and the Likert scale data to help her frame questions for her next piece of data gathering: one-to-one interviews.
iv. She discussed the questionnaires informally with some of the teachers who had completed them. This also gave her some ideas for the sort of questions to ask colleagues when she interviewed them.

As well as being informed by the questionnaires that each teacher had completed, Sam also went back to her original inquiry question and particularly focused on the second part of that question which looked at lesson planning. She therefore focused some of her questions on the differences in planning and approach to teaching an area of the science curriculum in which the teacher expressed greater confidence and one in which they expressed lesser confidence. She developed a series of questions as follows for her semi-structured interviews.

1. Can you talk me through the science topics that you have taught this academic year?
2. Which did you feel most/least confident about?
3. How did you go about planning the lessons in which you felt *least* confident?

4. How did you go about planning the lessons in which you felt *most* confident?
5. Is there anything else you feel I haven't asked you about this?

At various points, Sam asked colleagues to clarify or expand on what they had just said so that she could be reasonably sure that they had answered the question. Above all, she tried to make sure that these were relaxed interviews; so she didn't mind when teachers went 'off task' now and again: in fact she realized that this meant that the responses they were giving were more natural and hence probably more valid. Each of the interviews took about 20 minutes. Sam recorded each interview and took some notes. Sam read though her notes from each interview and listened back to each interview several times. In this way, she identified key themes that emerged from the interviews and she then went back to the recordings and transcribed short quotations from several sections of the interviews.

Thinking it through

- What do you think are the strengths and weaknesses of the methodology that Sam has chosen?
- What other approaches might she have adopted for this inquiry?
- What resource implications are there for supporting Sam during this inquiry? How could the school help this happen?

Presenting the inquiry

Sam's summative assessment for this module was in the form of a presentation to be given to staff at her school and submitted with notes to the university. Sam began her account of this inquiry with her findings. She started by making a short summary of what had emerged from her research data: from the questionnaires and the interviews. She wrote down what she had found: i) about teachers' confidence regarding subject knowledge; and ii) about their approach to planning and teaching science. She then wrote a short summary of what she had learnt from her reading around the literature on the subject. Looking at the two summaries Sam was able, with difficulty and with some help from a colleague and from her university tutor, to make some connections between what her data was telling her and what other researchers had previously found. This then provided Sam with the heart of her account of this inquiry: her own findings and how they related to the work of others.

Next, Sam wrote an introduction, focusing on those areas from the literature that she had found of most relevance for her findings in this inquiry. Finally, Sam wrote about the implications of her findings for herself and her school, this included: Sam's reflection upon her own subject knowledge and planning, what her findings suggested about the possible impact of teacher subject knowledge on children's learning and the school's future CPD needs in this respect.

Thinking it through

Sam collected a lot of data. How might she take this forward in future inquiries?

How could the school ensure that Sam's findings are disseminated across the school?

How might Sam's findings be developed by other colleagues?

How could the school management take Sam's findings forward as part of their action planning?

Case study: Inquiring into procedural subject knowledge

The context of the inquiry

Jack is a TLR holder with responsibility for history in an inner city 11–18 comprehensive in inner city Leeds. The school has four full time history teachers and there is currently one period of history each week lasting one hour for Years 7 to 9. There are two GCSE sets in Years 10 and 11 with three lessons of one hour and one set in Years 12 and 13 each with five hours per week of contact time. The number of pupils at the school opting for History has remained steady for the past three years as have exam results at KS4: the department achieved a GCSE average of 59 per cent A–C over three years. A level results in the past two years have, however, been declining and Jack has noticed that the pupils' ability to work with synoptic change at A2 is relatively weak.

The inquiry question

How well do Year 9 and 12 pupils understand the historical concepts of change and continuity and how might the department evolve practice to improve this?

Thinking it through

Consider the procedural knowledge that underpins your own subject, that is, how you go about doing it, the concepts and processes involved. How might you add to your own understanding of either pupil or teacher knowledge in these areas?

What data currently available in school might be helpful to undertake a study of this kind? How might undertaking this inquiry improve Jack's own subject knowledge for teaching?

The supporting literature

Jack examined the description and development of this concept through KS3 orders and the exam board descriptors. He then used practitioner literature from the journal *Teaching History* (www.history.org.uk) to identify some of the key issues surrounding change and continuity. Finally, he examined educational journals, including journals in Geography education where similar debates on change and continuity are current.

Thinking it through

How could Jack work with other TLR holders in the school to make this inquiry more collaborative in nature? For example, might he work with Geography or science specialists given that he has found literature on both of these subjects that helped inform his thinking? Share one piece of key reading about procedural knowledge that you have found in your own subject area.

The methodology

Jack decided to create a large data set by using all Year 9 pupils and Year 12 pupil currently studying history as his participant group. With such a large data set he did not want to use questionnaires because of the amount of work he felt this could entail but decided instead to undertake a detailed analysis of pupil work as his method of inquiry. His research question was broken down into three parts:

- What it the overall attainment level of Year 9 and 12 pupils in relation to the concept of change and continuity.
- Which aspects of change and continuity do pupils use in their answers currently? Description, extent, speed or nature?
- What differences are there if any between the Year 9 and 12 answers?

Generating the data

Jack wanted to work across all of the Year 9 and 12 classes within the school, not just his own. He therefore had to explain the purpose of his enquiry to all of the teachers of Years 9 and 12 and get their agreement to support his inquiry. As this was part of normal classroom duties, Jack did not need to get any ethical clearance from his university but he did check this with his tutor prior to beginning the study.

Jack set two benchmark tasks for pupils to complete on change and continuity: one for Year 9 and another for Year 12. Using practitioner-authored and research literature, Jack wanted to explore pupils' ability to analyse rather than merely describe change over time. He wanted to inquire into their understanding of speed, extent and nature of change over time in History. Jack analysed the pupils' responses along with other members of staff. They marked the work using a mark scheme provided by Jack and at a departmental meeting moderated the marking and gave feedback on overall pupil achievement during the task. Jack took in all the pupil work and did his own documentary analysis. Using four coloured pens, Jack highlighted text that was descriptive, text that analysed speed, extent or nature of change. To provide him with some further validation he asked two members of the department to look at five scripts and say whether they agreed or disagreed with his categorizations of the text.

Jack now had two sets of data, the overall attainment of the pupils using the mark scheme and a detailed textual analysis of the nature of their answers. Jack compared the two sets of data examining the overall attainment of ten individual pupils in Year 9 and five pupils in Year 12 with their detailed breakdown of the answers. Jack was also able to examine the nature and extent of progress between Year 9 and 12 in both overall attainment and in the nature of their individual answers.

Thinking it through

Although Jack did not require ethical clearance, what potential ethical issues might be highlighted by this approach?

How could this inquiry be adapted to inform your own department's understanding of either pupil or teacher procedural knowledge?

How could Jack have gone about this inquiry using different methods?

How did Jack try to ensure reliability and validity in his study? How effective do you judge his attempts to do this?

Presenting the Inquiry

Jack was required to produce a report as part of his summative assessment; he had to write a list of key recommendations for future practice as part of this report. He began by presenting his overall findings in the form of pie charts. These showed the proportion of pupils achieving at each level of attainment in the task overall and then in both Years 9 and 12 separately. Jack then presented pie charts showing the percentage of answers that contained some element of description and those that contained analysis of change using speed, extent or nature. Again, these were given overall in the first instance and then broken down into Years 9 and 12 subsequently. Having first described his findings, Jack went on to give some analysis of the findings; the links between overall attainment and the nature of the answers given; the differences between Years 9 and 12 in both attainment and answers. Jack used literature to provide some context for the findings: how typical were they? How did they compare with findings by other teachers or researchers? Jack used verbatim examples of 'pupil speak' from the 15 scripts he had analysed in detail to illustrate his points. Finally, he presented a plan of action for the department that linked clearly to his findings and a timeline for its implementation.

In the appendices for the submitted assignment, Jack included the anonymized 15 scripts of the individual pupils, copies of the two bench mark tasks and the mark scheme and lesson plan given to the teachers.

Thinking it through

How could Jack build upon this work in future practice either within a masters or as part of departmental development work?

How could Jack disseminate this work in the school and who should be the audience? Fellow History teachers? Pupils? Teachers from outside the department? The senior management team?

Jack might present his work in a practitioner journal or at a conference. What can you see as the benefits and challenges of this?

Drawing it together

Subject knowledge is an enormous area for potential inquiry. In this chapter, we have shown one way of approaching this: investigating substantive and procedural knowledge and examining each from a different perspective. Sam investigated teachers' knowledge and Jack explored pupils' knowledge; both were conceived as a way in which to inform teachers' knowledge. Each approached their inquiry in different ways but both generated insights that they will be able to use to shape both their practice and the way in which they engage with inquiry in the future.

References

DEE (1999) *science: The National Curriculum for England.* London: HMSO.

Ellis, V. (2007) *Subject Knowledge and Teacher Education.* London: Continuum.

Guyver, R. and Nichols, J. (2004) From novice to effective teacher: a study of postgraduate training and history pedagogy. *International Journal of Historical Learning, Teaching and Research,* Vol. 4, No. 1, pp. 177–94.

Lee, P., Ashby, R. and Dickinson, A. (1997) Research methods and some findings on rational understanding, in O'Neill, C. and Pendry, A. (eds.) *Principles and Practice: Analytical Perspectives On Curriculum Reform and Changing Pedagogy from History Teacher Educators.* Lancaster: SCHTE.

Richardson, I. (2006) What is good science education? in Wood-Robinson, V. (Ed.) *ASE Guide to science Education.* Hatfield: Association for science Education.

Shulman, L. (1987) Knowledge and teaching: Foundations of the new reform. *Harvard Educational Review,* Vol. 57, No. 1, pp. 1–22.

Turner-Bissett, R. (2001) *Expert Teaching: Knowledge and Pedagogy to Lead the Profession.* London: David Fulton.

6 Inquiring into Children's Development and Behaviour

Dean Pearson

Chapter Outline

Introduction

The process of teaching and learning does not exist in a vacuum. There are a number of other factors that have a substantive impact on children's behaviour and development. In this chapter we will examine a range of these factors and highlight some of the research that has contributed to our understanding of how these factors can intersect to shape the learning experiences of individual children. Initiatives such as Every Child Matters have drawn the attention of teachers to the need to individualize teaching and learning experiences. Teachers are encouraged to embrace the holistic nature of teaching and learning and acknowledge that this process will vary from child to child depending on a range of cognitive, social, emotional and physical factors; this chapter aims to show how you can enhance and develop your knowledge and understanding of these factors through classroom inquiry.

Thinking it through

Discuss your understanding of the following factors and their impact on behaviour and development, you could think about traffic lighting your confidence in the following:

- Cognitive; what understanding do you have of specific cognitive impairments? How might theories such as learning styles impact on your practice? What do you understand about language acquisition for EAL pupils?
- Social/cultural; how might factors such as class orientation or ethnicity impact on learning? What is your understanding of this?
- Emotional: how could self esteem impact on learning? Anxiety? What do you know about this?
- Physical: what impact does the physical environment have on learning? The room layout? Lighting? To what extent do you consider this and what do you know?

Record red for areas you know little or nothing about, orange for areas you have some but limited knowledge of and green for those in which you feel confident.

Reading about influences on development and behaviour

There is a huge body of educational research which investigates factors influencing development and behaviour, but as with many things in life it is easier to describe the changes than to explain them. Children change all the time, albeit not always (if ever!) on a simple, smooth and predictable upwards curve. Psychologists have divided these changes into two categories; *transformational* change and *variational* change (Margaret Harris, 2008). As they move from infancy to adulthood, children undergo huge transformational changes that are physical, cognitive, social and emotional and these are often interrelated.

Variational change refers to the smaller scale changes within children's overall development at particular points in time. Children's development can and does vary from day to day and even within a lesson: for example, studies show how children's strategies for problem solving vary from day to day, one day they may use their fingers to count on and the next recall the answer without using fingers (Margaret Harris and George Butterworth 2002). Some children at a similar developmental stage may have better reading than others. Variational change is how this is accounted for.

As teachers you will have clearly seen both kinds of change, the transformational as children age and the variational between children and within a single child. Describing them is the easy part: our role as inquiring teachers needs to be to examine our role in those changes, especially the variational. We can do little about the transformational but how might the processes of teaching and learning we control within the classroom impact upon the variational?

Clearly this a huge area of research in the educational and psychological fields and what follows is not an attempt to cover all of the research in great depth, rather it provides an overview of some which might help you to identify and frame areas of personal interest and from there find further reading and develop an inquiry question.

Our initial starting points are some of the broad theories of teaching and learning. These help to form a good basis for an inquiry because they prepare us for what we might be seeing as we observe in the classroom. Early theories of the nature of intelligence prompted educationalists to see the human mind as a *tabula rasa* or blank slate, implying that children's minds could be simply opened and information conveniently inserted and assimilated. It was Jean Piaget who led a vanguard of thinkers proposing a quite different view of the nature of the teaching and learning process. Piaget's famous theory of cognitive development insisted that the ability to learn was dependent on which stage of development a child was at. A number of experiments into object permanence, egocentricity and a child's ability to conserve by number mass and volume revealed exactly what could be learnt at a particular stage in early life. Piaget identified four broad developmental stages ranging from birth to adolescence, these included: *the sensory motor; the pre-operational; the concrete operational and the formal operational stages* (Jean Piaget 1954).

Undoubtedly, Piaget's approach has had a huge impact on the world of education but it would serve us well to investigate more contemporary assumptions about the nature of teaching and learning.

Humanism

This approach was pioneered by the American psychologist Carl Rogers and is characterized by the phrase 'student centred learning'. Rogers had five principles of learning underpinning his theories:

1. One person cannot directly 'teach' another person, they can only facilitate their learning.
2. A person only significantly learns that which enhances them; they have to see the relevance to themselves.
3. People resist new knowledge that requires them to make changes to the ways in which they see themselves; open mindedness is therefore crucial to learning.
4. Resistance to changes to the self become stronger when under any threat; open, friendly classrooms are therefore essential.
5. Effective education can happen best when the threat to the learner's concept of self is reduced to the minimum and different ways of thinking are presented that connect the learner to the learning (Rogers, 1951).

Humanism's key principles therefore suggest that teachers should be seen as facilitators who guide children's learning by connecting it with their experience and making it relevant to them. Rogers believed that teaching should be empathetic and sensitive and focused on the development of positive self-concepts within children. Humanism advocates the empowerment of learners through active engagement with decision making processes and further argues that only this produces 'meaningful learning': learning which has personal meaning and is therefore embedded and lasting. Rogers argues that other forms of teaching can produce 'meaningless learning', characterized by rote recall and testing. This is 'learning from the neck up', it has no connection with the feelings and self of the learner.

Thinking it through

Carl Rogers theories evolved during the 1950s and 1960s. How relevant do you think the humanist view of learning is in your school today?

How does this theory compare with those of constructivism and behaviourism in Chapter 4?

How might you generate an inquiry question that explores these theories? For example, how much do you try to connect learning to the learner? How much facilitating do you do as opposed to directing learning?

Are children learning 'from the neck up'? Can you explore evidence of embedded learning as envisaged by the humanists? How might this link to variational changes in development?

Learning styles

Other theorists have examined the learning styles of individuals and their potential impact on development and behaviour. Rita Dunn et al. (1996) identified a learning style inventory with five categories:

1. Environmental style: the layout of the room the lighting, displays and so on.
2. Emotional style: concerning motivation, persistence, structure and responsibility.
3. Sociological: learning by self, with peers, with an adult.
4. Physiological: time of day, mobility, food and drink.
5. Psychological: competition or cooperation, impulsive or reflective.

Others such as Peter Honey and Alan Mumford (2000) propose four categories of learners:

- Reflector: prefers to learn from activities that allow them to watch, think and review what has happened.
- Theorist: prefers to think problems through in a step-by-step manner.
- Pragmatist: prefers to apply new learning to practice to see if they work.
- Activist: prefers the challenges of new experiences, involvement with others, assimilation and role-playing (Honey and Mumford, 2000).

Thinking it through

Learning styles have been influential in some schools in recent times: visual auditory and kinaesthetic, for example, or Gardner's multiple intelligences (1985). How have you been influenced by them in your classroom?

To what extent might learning style in children be subject to variational and transformational change? Does it depend on age? Could that type of task influence the preferred style? For example, might learning preference change if the task was to bake a cake as opposed to solving a maths puzzle?

Can you observe the influence of learning styles in teaching or in the response of your learners?

Socio-cultural influences

The influence of socio-cultural factors on development and behaviour is hard to overestimate. They powerfully shape the teaching and learning process and pupils' perception of school. Paul Willis' seminal 1977 study examined why working-class boys ended up in working class jobs and found evidence of the development of an anti-school culture among teenage working-class boys which appeared to be influenced by the home environment and was characterized by resistance to middle class values often propagated by the school, but also by lack of aspiration. Shirley Griggs and Rita Dunn (1996) identified ethnic and cultural differences in the learning styles of different cultural groups and Jo Boaler's (1997) work explored the underlying reasons for girls' underachievement in mathematics. Boaler's work may be a good starting point for investigating gender variables in performance and behaviour.

Physical influences

Nigel Hastings and Karen Chantrey-Woods (2002) examine how the arrangement of desks within the primary classroom impacts upon teaching and learning and argues against group tables as a form of standard practice. Walter Creekmore (1987) explores the influence of classroom walls on learning and behaviour; he suggests that the learning and development of children, including those with special educational needs, can be enhanced by three different kinds of classroom wall display.

- Acquisition display: placed at the front, holding the blackboard/whiteboard and the class notice board. Only new concepts or ones that the children are struggling with should be placed here.
- Maintenance display: to go at the sides of the classroom. Material on these walls has already been covered and helps pupils to fully understand the concepts.
- Dynamic display: placed at the back; containing students' work, temporary notices, Christmas decorations, etc.

Thinking it through

All inquiries have ethical considerations that must be taken into account. What are the particular ethical considerations of exploring socio-cultural issues such as gender, class or race? Does this mean that these issues should not be explored?

The area of development and behaviour is clearly huge; this chapter has only been able to comment on a few of the many studies that have been undertaken in this area and there are others that have not been touched upon such as those on: teacher expectation, the impact of setting on behaviour, motivation, or the effect of strategies designed to alter or improve behaviour to name but a few. What is important is that as a result of your prior experience, your school setting and your own reading, you identify an area for inquiry that is both manageable and helps you to alter and develop your own teaching and learning.

Framing your question

The next stage in generating an inquiry question is considering which issues to focus upon in the myriad of possibilities in the areas of development and behaviour: some will have to be disregarded or postponed until a later inquiry. It is also important to try and isolate themes within a question. Choose overlapping themes in this area and you run the risk of acquiring too much data, making interpreting and presenting so much more difficult. For example, in a question that explores classroom layout, the addition of a second focus on learning styles would potentially be confusing. Which of the two factors is associated with the impact you are seeing? How do you then interpret the data you gather in?

Thinking it through

- Identify an area you think you would like to look at. How does this area matter to you as a teacher? To your school?
- Revisit the possible factors that impact upon development and behaviour; physical, cognitive, emotional etc, are there any gender or ethnicity aspects that would make a comparative study a possibility? What reading can you use to help explore and refine these issues?
- What methodology(s) will you be considering? What practical considerations are thrown up by this?
- How can your key concepts be operationalized? How can you define your terms to provide clarity? What are you 'measuring'?

Case study: Exploring gender effects

Context of the inquiry

Paul was in his fifth year of teaching. He was a humanities teacher who had recently acquired a responsibility for coordinating the KS4 curriculum. His school in the North East of England was an 11–16 mixed comprehensive with one thousand on roll. GCSE results for A–C passes including English and maths were regularly below the 50 per cent mark. One of Paul's responsibilities was the analysis of exam results at KS4, and he noticed a number of anomalies that occur in attainment levels with regard to gender. Paul particularly noted that in general terms, boys' achievement was lower than that of girls; he also noticed that in other areas of the school curriculum there was a pattern where girls' achievement had seen a steadily downward trend in recent years, identifying science and maths in particular in this respect.

Furthermore, Paul had also observed a number of gender-related patterns connected to subject choice at the end of Year 9 with boys tending to lean towards Technology and ICT while the uptake for languages and the arts were much higher among girls. There was also a distinct gender imbalance with regard to the humanities, with take up for History, Geography and RE being quite heavily weighted in favour of girls.

Paul began to think about the impact of variables such as gender on the teaching and learning process. In particular, he suspected that whole school policies and practices and indeed those of individual departments and subject teachers may inadvertently have either overstated gender differences or more significantly, reinforced gender stereotypes. This in turn he proposed may have been in part responsible for the range of anomalies he observed with regard to attainment.

The inquiry question

Paul had a number of informal discussions with members of his own department about these issues and he was fully au fait with recent government initiatives aimed at promoting positive gender images in schools and raising boys' achievement. With this in mind he initially posed the following question.

To what extent does the school construct gender differences by associating certain characteristics to one gender over another and then acting accordingly?

Thinking it through

Are there any ethical issues with regard to a question of this nature?

How might such sensitive topics be handled effectively?

Given that there are likely to be a number of other variables which intersect with gender to influence the teaching and learning process, how do you make research proposals such as this manageable? How do you either limit and or isolate your data to enable you to make generalizations from your results?

What are likely to be whole school outcomes as a result of research like this? How will it inform school practice? Will it have an impact on school culture? Is it likely to affect the everyday practices of individuals? In short where is an inquiry like this going?

The supporting literature

Paul's initial starting point were the many pieces of research with which he was familiar in the psychology of education. He began by revisiting work investigating biological differences that are likely to impact on performance; for example, Jeffrey Gray and Anthony Buffery (1971) cite the dominance of left and right hemisphere activity in the brain as a possible explanation for girls developing greater skills of verbal reasoning while boys develop a greater aptitude for spatial and mathematical tasks.

Paul thought about the influence of the home environment and questioned the role of the socialization process by re-reading Jane Pilcher's (1999) claim that boys and girls enter the education process looking and behaving in gender appropriate ways. Although this research is relevant in terms of foundation thinking, Paul felt that the influence of the school was also a major factor and so he refamiliarized himself with work investigating this area. Of the many studies available, he was drawn to Katharine Clarricoate's (1980) claim that teacher expectations follow gender stereotyped patterns, or Best's (1993) suggestion that a good deal of reading material available in schools promotes typical gender roles. Although able to access national data on academic performance as related to gender, Paul was more interested in a case study approach and so revisited Feylsa Demie's 2001 study looking into gender differences in achievement and implications for school improvement.

Despite the fact that Paul's imagination was stimulated by these studies, he felt they did not really offer a tangible peg on which to hang a research methodology for his own work; at this point he decided to investigate the Department for Children, Schools and Families' document of 2009: 'Gender issues in schools – what works to improve attainment for boys and girls' (DCSF 2009).

Methodology

The DCFS publication was keen to stress the importance of whole school strategies to promote positive gender images, these include the following:

- Behaviour management policy.
- The development of strategies for equal opportunities.
- The installation of policies regarding shared values.
- The promotion of strategies to promote pupil involvement in the life of the school.

Again Paul believed these to be a little too vague to inform a coherent methodology but then noticed the section entitled 'action plans' and it is at this point that workable ideas begin to appear, as did potential methodological frames. Paul was interested in five areas in particular:

Action plan one

This asked the question: *Do images and concepts within the physical school environment bring out clear gender differences?* Research in this area lends itself to visual methodologies and Paul imagined a video or photographic project undertaken by students investigating gender perceptions prompted by the school environment.

Action plan two

This asked the questions: *What expectations and perceptions of femininity and masculinity form a part of the school fabric? What practices expectations and roles prevail?* Paul believed that a similar methodology would serve these questions well and that form periods, assemblies and school productions could be promising observation foci.

Action plan three

This posed the question: *What are the current expectations of teachers regarding gender?* Paul considered qualitative methods and an interview schedule as possible methods for this inquiry.

Action plan four

This was led by the question: *Are there patterns which emerge in relation to individual subject areas?* For example, are there different expectations of performance in say science or maths? Paul visualized a series of observations in a variety of different curriculum areas and began to think about a possible coding framework for his observation.

Action plan five

The key question here was: *Do boys and girls follow specific routes of study at the end of Year 9?* Paul did not want to neglect the power of quantitative data for reflecting patterns and trends and so investigated how he might access internal school data on subject choice and or indeed national data.

Thinking it through

Given that you may have a full teaching timetable how do you think this will impact on your choice of research method?

What are likely to be time issues connected to the use of qualitative methods? How do you intend to facilitate observations or interview schedules in practical terms?

Are there any methods that you have considered which require specific materials? Is your school able to provide these materials?

Have you considered issues of access to the data you require? You may need the co-operation of a number of parties in your work. How important is it to operationalize concepts which you investigate? In what way might we define concepts so they can be measured?

How could visual methods such as photographs be used with younger children? Where would you look to find out more about this methodology?

Paul initially considered combining methods but was aware of the danger of acquiring too much data and thus potentially leaving his work in danger of being criticized for being too thin and lacking in depth. For this reason, Paul chose to collaborate with a group of Year 11 students to produce a photographic and video presentation on notions of gender within the school, closely related to action plans one and two from the government document which had informed his methodology.

Paul employed the support of the ICT and Personal Social Health and Religious Education (PSHRE) departments and selected two small groups of girls: one group to be responsible for video evidence, the other photographic evidence. He then did the same with two groups of boys. Paul wanted to avoid being overprescriptive as this could overinfluence the data his participants generated; however, he felt he needed to suggest the following areas as worthy of investigation:

- school notice boards
- awards boards
- assemblies
- playground spaces
- form periods.

Paul decided to keep the research questions simple and accessible to the participants and so briefed them with simplified versions of the following:

> What evidence of feminine and masculine identity do you see emerging from the school environment?
> What messages about gender are being conveyed through the school environment?
> What gender roles are in evidence, are they positive negative or stereotyped?

Presenting the inquiry

Paul allowed the students one week to collect evidence, after which the results were presented on three levels. Initially their work was used in PSHRE lessons to stimulate discussion on gender inequalities. Secondly, the presentations were given to Paul's fellow students and tutor at the university with some detailed analysis of the content and some conclusions drawn. Thirdly, Paul sought permission to present his findings on a whole staff inset day with a view to stimulating colleagues to begin the process of developing strategies to address gender based underachievement in school.

Thinking it through

What are some of the advantages and disadvantages of working with students as co-researchers?

What ethical considerations can you think of in connection with this sort of inquiry?

What about issues of reliability and validity?

Case study: Active learning

Context of inquiry

Katie works in a primary school with 150 pupils in a semi-rural area. She is in her third year of teaching and has a Year 5 class. There are two full-time classroom assistants, both attached to specific pupils with statements but who work with groups of pupils as well. Katie had observed that there was a wide range of differentiation in the learning environment created by the experienced teachers she had observed. These included differences in seating arrangements, general classroom layout, even the management of light and colour within individual rooms. Katie wanted to be able to use the classroom environment more effectively, especially to promote better behaviour with key pupils she was finding difficult to manage. Katie's Key Stage leader was keen to promote active learning, especially discovery learning among Key Stage 2 children and although Katie wished to embrace child-centred teaching and learning, she was very aware of the noise levels in her classroom when she was doing this. She also worried about the number of children potentially off-task for a significant percentage of the time.

Supporting literature

Katie was somewhat surprised when her initial reading showed that the relationship between noise, performance and behaviour was not clear-cut. She began with a study conducted across a cross-section of London primaries in 2003 by Bridget Shield and Julie Dockrell: this argued that high noise levels significantly impaired cognitive ability. Another study by Christie and Glickman (1980), however, argued that there was no difference in cognitive abilities with varying noise levels. Sydney Zentall (1983) found that loud music in a classroom reduced disruptive behaviour with hyperactive children but left children on the autistic spectrum passive.

With this conflicting research base, Katie decided to focus on her own class and begin by initially assessing the amount if time they actually were spending off task.

Inquiry question

Do noise levels have any impact upon on task and off task behaviours?

Methodology

Katie decided that the first stage of her proposal would be to operationalize what she meant by off task behaviour. Some of her ideas included:

- getting out of their seats;
- moving around the room;
- non-task-related conversation lasting more than one minute
- lack of focus on the task for longer than three minutes
- abandoning the task.

Katie realized that she had two options when coding her observations: event recording where, for example, she noted every time a child moved around the room; or time recording, when she recorded the time that children were off-task and did not code what it was they were doing off task. A third option would be to combine these two coding methods. Katie wanted to use a quantitative methodology which she felt would be easier to analyse and good for making comparisons and spotting patterns.

Thinking it through

What are some of the challenges when observing while teaching?

How might you mitigate these challenges through your choice of sample size?

What other strategies might you adopt to help with observation of your own practice?

Katie wanted to ensure that the observations were as discrete and unobtrusive as possible. She firstly broke down the 24 children in the class into small groups which would become the focus of her observations. She worked with her teaching assistants to involve them in the inquiry; they discussed the coding system she had designed and undertook a joint initial dry run to make sure that it worked for all three of them. The observations occurred as Katie and the TAs were working with the pupils across a range of lessons from formal didactic teaching of numeracy to the project based independent learning. Katie also set up a small video camera within the room to record the lessons. Each observer focused on eight children.

Presenting the inquiry

Katie had gathered a lot of quantitative data showing the time spent off task and she matched this to the time within the lesson and the noise levels as recorded on the video. She presented this in a number of bar charts and histograms. These were discussed with her TAs and with the Key Stage manager.

> ### Thinking it through
>
> Classrooms frequently have more than one adult in them; how could you use these additional people to help gather data for your own inquiry?
>
> Katie's study is quite reliant on her own perceptions; of on- task and off-task behaviour, of noise. Consider how working with other adults can help to explore and refine some of these subjective perceptions.

Bringing it together

Attempting to isolate variables which impact upon classroom performance and behaviour is indeed a daunting task. It is only sensible to conclude that the cognitive, physical, socio-cultural and emotional elements intersect to produce a complex collage of potential influences on the teaching and learning process and the behaviour of children. This process is widely recognized by those who have produced research in the field and should also be acknowledged by those engaging in research at M level. That is not to say, however, that engaging in inquiry in these areas should be seen as a no win process unlikely to produce reliable and valid results and as such best avoided. One might argue rather that practising teachers have a significant role to play in adding to the body of knowledge in this area. In terms of methodologies, it is to be hoped that what has emerged from this chapter is that in what is a very complex field 'less' is very often 'more'.

References

Best, l. (1993) Dragons, dinner ladies and ferrets: sex roles in children's books. *Sociology Review*, Vol. 2, No. 3, pp. 6–8.

Boaler, J. (1997) *Experiencing School mathematics: Teaching Styles, Sex and Setting*. Buckingham: Open University Press.

Christie, D.J. and Glickman, C.D. (1980). The effects of classroom noise on children: Evidence for sexual differences. *Psychology in the Schools,* Vol. 17, No. 3, pp. 405–8.

Clarricoates, K. (1980) 'The importance of being Ernest. . . Emma . . . Tom . . . Jane: the perception and categorisation of gender conformity and gender deviation in primary schools' in Deem, R. (ed.) (1980) *Schooling for Women's Work.* London: Routledge and Kegan Paul.

Creekmore, W. (1987) Effective use of classroom walls. *Academic Therapy,* Vol. 22, No. 4, pp. 143–53.

Demie, F. (2001) Ethnic and gender differences in educational achievement and implications for school improvement strategies. *Educational Research,* Vol. 43, No. 1, pp. 91–106.

Department for Schools, Children and Families (2009) *Gender Issues in Schools-What Works to Improve Attainment for Boys and Girls.* London: HMSO. Available at http://media.education.gov.uk/assets/files/pdf/8/8311dcsfgender%20what%20works%20bmkpdf.pdf (Accessed 31/8/11).

Dunn, R., Dunn, K. and Price, G. E. (1996*). Learning Style Inventory.* Lawrence, KS: Price Systems.

Gardner, H. (1985) *Frames of Mind: The Theory of Multiple Intelligences.* New York: Basic Books.

Gray, J. and Buffery, A. (1971) Sex differences, emotional and cognitive behaviour in mammals including man: adaptive and neural bases. *Acta Psychologia,* Vol. 35, pp. 89–111.

Griggs, S. and Dunn, R. (1996) Hispanic-American students and learning style. *Emergency Librarian,* Vol. 23, No. 2, p. 11.

Harris, M. and Butterworth, G. (2002) *Developmental Psychology.* Hove: Psychology Press.

Harris, M. (2008) *Exploring Developmental Psychology: Understanding Theory and Methods.* London: Sage.

Hastings, N. and Chantrey-Woods, K. (2002) *Reorganising Primary Classroom.* Buckingham: Open University Press.

Honey, P. and Mumford, A. (2000). *The Learning Styles Helper's Guide.* P Maidenhead: Peter Honey Publications.

Piaget, J. (1954) *The Construction of Reality in the Child.* London: Routledge.

Piaget, J. (1969) *The Mechanisms of Perception.* New York: Basic Books.

Pilcher, J. (1999*) Women in Contemporary Britain: An Introduction.* London: Routledge.

Rogers, C. (1951) *Client-Centered Therapy: Its Current Practice, Implications and Theory.* London: Constable.

Shield, B. and Dockrell, J. (2003) The effects of noise on the attainments and cognitive performance of primary school children. *Executive Summary Report.* London: South Bank University.

Willis, P. (1977) *Learning to Labour.* Aldershot: Gower.

Zentall, S. (1983) Learning Environments: a review of physical and temporal factors. *Exceptional Educational Quarterly,* Vol. 4, pp. 90–115.

Inquiring into Inclusion

Melanie Garlick, Cath Lawes and Katie Hall

Introduction

Walk into any classroom and you will see children taking part in what is going on in many different ways. Observe children when they are out of the classroom and you will see how and with whom they play or spend their time. Ask children about how they are learning at school: is the pace of lessons too fast or too slow? Are they always waiting for others, or struggling to keep up? Consider how some pupils' experience of the classroom is almost entirely shaped by the way they work with adult helpers. Look at how children with disabilities participate in physical education. How do children for whom English is a second language access the curriculum? How and when should we decide that children should be educated in specialist provision?

All of these are aspects of inclusion, a term with which you are no doubt familiar, although we hope in the pages that follow to challenge your understanding of the term. This chapter is concerned with thinking carefully about what inclusion means, providing some ideas for how you can inquire into inclusion in your setting and helping you to weigh up what your inquiry findings might suggest about practices in which you are involved.

Inclusion

What is inclusion? Margaret Reynolds (1989) suggests that inclusion is best regarded as a progressive trend for taking increasing responsibility for educating groups previously excluded from mainstream society. Inclusion can, she writes, perhaps be described as a vision in which all children and young people will be happy, healthy, enjoy and achieve; be part of an inclusive community which works cohesively; attend the same school as their friends and neighbours and feel completely included.

Inclusion can have many faces: it can mean a place, a curriculum, a particular form of support, an intervention or a grouping of pupils. In the end, however, it really means a *feeling*: pupils that are included have a sense of belonging in a school or college that others who feel excluded, left out or marginalized do not enjoy. This raises an immediate practical issue for you in your inquiries into inclusion: feelings, especially when they are sensitive and personal, are naturally difficult to explore. Later in this chapter we will give suggestions for how you can work around this difficulty but for now bear in mind that while inclusion may be challenging to research, it can also go to the heart of what schools genuinely achieve for pupils. Children who feel excluded are failed by the system just as much as those who do not succeed academically and they are often, of course, the same pupils.

It is important for you to think about your own personal view of inclusion but it's also vital to gain a wider perspective through your reading. Exploring what others have written about inclusion and reviewing recent legislation will provides you with a important starting point for your inquiry and we shall turn to that next.

Thinking it through

What does 'inclusion' mean to you?

Has this first section made you think any differently about what inclusion means?

Have your views on inclusion changed over the course of your career? If so, why do you think that is? Try to identify key experiences that have affected your views.

What has been written about inclusion?

Principles

The idea of inclusion means different things to different people, including those who over the years have written on the subject. There is a thorough discussion around the development of notions of inclusion in Norah Frederickson and Tony Cline (2009) among other places, so what we will do here is to help point up some of the key areas in these debates in order to help you to think through your inquiry. We will start with the debates on the essential definition of inclusion and move towards the more pragmatic, contextual points as we go through.

First, inclusion has been seen by many as a human right. Pupils have a certain entitlement to a similar education to that of their peers. Recognizing this, the Salamanca World Statement (UNESCO 1994) called on governments:

> . . . to adopt the principles of inclusive education, enrolling all children in regular schools unless there are compelling reasons for doing otherwise' (p. 44).

The Centre for Studies in Inclusive Education elaborated on this line of thought in 2004, arguing that 'there are no legitimate reasons to separate children for their education' (CSIE 2004), and giving inclusion a broad rationale by stating the principle that an integrated education is the best preparation for life in a pluralistic world.

Here, the human rights strand in inclusion begins to merge into what we might call the 'good society' argument: that inclusive education has the potential both to foster tolerance of diversity in the wider community and to help integration of those with, for example, disabilities or learning difficulties in society. Schools should and do, in some senses, reflect the world of which they are a part and segregated education can be seen a an cause or effect of a segregated society (sectarian education in Northern Ireland is an obvious example here).

So you might well take from what you've read so far in this section that there is a powerful moral argument for inclusive education, but as I'm sure you will appreciate, we will never have an education system that is entirely inclusive in all the senses we discussed at the start of this chapter and however inclusive your own setting, there will always be questions to ask about how and how profoundly pupils are included. Nevertheless, thinking about how these overarching principles interact with your own convictions and the pragmatic, resource-limited world of education in which you find yourself is a good starting point for planning your investigation. For example, the CSIE argument here would be important in helping you think about how inclusion can affect children's life chances beyond school. Should our view of inclusion be limited to what happens to a child up to the age of sixteen? How do inclusive classrooms impact on 'mainstream children'?

Changing schools, changing pupils

When you read about inclusion, you'll sometimes see it contrasted with *integration*. This was a term used before the 1990s to describe the placement of children with learning difficulties or disabilities in mainstream schools. Put simply, integration implies that the pupil should adapt to the school in which they are placed whereas inclusion, in contrast, places the onus on the school to change to meet the needs of the pupil. Inclusion involves the school in adapting curricula, methods, materials and procedures: restructuring to embrace all children. Integration involves assimilation of the individual, making changes so that the Special Educational Needs (SEN) pupil can 'fit in'. This is surely far more than a case of one word being replaced by another, there is a clear distinction between the two terms and that distinction is based on theoretical notions of how we view children.

Richard Rieser and Micheline Mason (1992) argue that medical advances which have 'cured' many physical and mental conditions have disposed us to think in terms of similar 'solutions' for those with physical or learning difficulties. While this may appear a 'common sense' attitude; it has quite pernicious consequences if we begin to see the general population as 'normal' and those with impairments as somehow in need of treatment and somehow therefore lesser than others without the same difficulties. Rieser and Mason theorize that there is a *medical* and a *social* model of thinking about physical and learning difficulties. The medical model way of thinking tends to label the individual according to their impairment and by implication regards that individual as in some way faulty just as we would rather the ill were cured. If only we could find the magic bullet, these children would be like everybody else. In contrast, the social model tends not to 'other' people who are not 'normal' and to define individuals on their own terms, not through some objectification of their abilities. This model of thinking is inherently more accepting of plurality.

In similar vein, Susan Hart et al. (2007) review studies that show that teachers can have their expectations powerfully shaped by the labelling of pupils as having special or additional educational needs. You may wish to explore labelling and its effects as part of your inquiry. One dilemma of inclusion is that children identified with a particular need are more likely to receive additional educational resources but are equally more likely to be treated as 'different'. Looking at the sometimes subtle ways in which some pupils are perceived as different by their peers and by teachers would be an interesting basis for an inquiry.

Seeing inclusion

In the inquiries that you may carry out, you will likely be looking for evidence of inclusion in your setting. However complex inclusion is an a concept, it is possible to *operationalize*: that is, to choose a particular definition and then try to relate that definition to the sorts of behaviour you might observe and the sort of data you might generate. To help you think in this way, we present here a brief summary of some of the literature on what inclusion looks like.

Mel Ainscow (2007) offers a very simple means of evaluating inclusion by focusing on pupil outcomes in three respects: *presence*, including attendance; *participation*, including a sense of belonging; and *achievement*. This approach is expanded into a broader and more comprehensive rubric in the Index for Inclusion (Booth and Ainscow 2011). The approach the authors take in this comprehensive work is to provide a framework that is in effect a description of inclusion in action based on an appreciation of the inclusive values that underlie these actions. You may find this document useful in informing the way in which you structure your observations: helping you to judge in a more sophisticated way exactly how the practice you see relates to notions of inclusion.

A really interesting piece of work by Luanna Meyer et al. (1998) provides another way of looking at inclusion. The authors present a perspective for appreciating the extent to which pupils are *socially* included. They describe some pupils, for example as 'ghosts and guests' in the school: in contrast, for example, another category they suggest is 'just another kid'. It's worth reiterating here that the point of such theoretical insights is not necessarily the privileged view of 'the truth' that they offer us: you should see them as a tool that can help you see past the surface appearance of things in a setting with which you may be very familiar, helping you to see afresh and perhaps notice what you might otherwise overlook.

We have given a very brief and partial overview here of the literature on inclusion. This is a subject on which a great deal has been written and there is a lot of specialist literature – for example, in relation to particular SEN diagnoses – that might be helpful for your particular study. As a general resource and starting point for your reading, Frederickson and Cline (2009) is one of the most comprehensive texts around.

In the next section we briefly consider the policy context of inclusion.

Thinking it through

Your first reaction to reading this might well be 'yes but . . .'. In your experience, can all children be included in your setting?

What about children with behavioural difficulties? Would you categorize their right to inclusion any differently to that of other pupils?

Legislation, guidance and inclusion

In many institutions, concern with legislation around SEN and inclusion might well be considered to be the preserve of the Special Needs or Inclusion Coordinator although it's important for all teachers to have some understanding in this area. For you as an inquirer, some knowledge in this area is helpful because government and other 'official' publications are often suggestive of wider values in education and society and because the requirements of legislation will inevitably shape thinking within your organization.

The British government has for many years expressed support for the principle of inclusion (DfEE, 1997) indicating that the aim, wherever possible, should be to educate children in the mainstream, hence increasing the skills and resources available for all pupils in mainstream schools (note that this is another way you might argue in favour of inclusion: it has a part to play in supporting mainstream schools). At the same time, however, a commitment has continued to maintain specialist provision (including Special Schools) for pupils whose individual needs could not *reasonably* be met in mainstream schools. The Special Educational Needs and Disability Act 2001 delivered a strengthened right to a mainstream education for children with Special Educational Needs. This document amended the Education Act 1996 and transformed the statutory framework into a positive endorsement of inclusion. The Act sought to enable more pupils to be included successfully within mainstream education and marked an important change in provision by making it unlawful to discriminate against pupils on the basis of their disability.

The Children Act of 2004 introduced a five-point universal entitlement framework for children in the form of Every Child Matters (ECM), moving the focus to early intervention, information sharing and integrated front-line services. Although it appears at the time of writing that the ECM framework is to be reviewed, the five headings remain a helpful structure for considering all aspects of inclusion as you can read in case study 3 below.

A number of commissions have since evaluated aspects of inclusion, most notably the Bercow report (2008) on speech language and communication; the Lamb Inquiry (2009) on parental confidence in the SEN framework; the Salt review (2010) on the supply of specialist teachers; and most recently, the Ofsted special educational needs and disability review (Ofsted, 2010), which included the influential judgement that too many pupils were being identified as 'SEN' whose needs could simply be met through 'good teaching'. Most recently at the time of writing, the Green Paper of 2011 proposed reforms and simplifications of the SEN system and contained a simple but radial statement that 'we will remove the bias towards inclusion' (DfE, 2011, 5). The consequences of this statement have yet to be felt but if this recommendation begins to inform policy then this publication will have marked a significant change in direction with regards to inclusion in this country.

Uncertainty around inclusion, however, did not start with the recent Green Paper. Geoff Lindsay (2003) found that policy towards inclusion in the UK was well advanced, but not all encompassing. Specifically, the ambiguities in government documents in the past decade over whether 'inclusion' refers to all or simply most students have resulted in a variety of interpretations. For example, the series of surveys by the Centre for Studies on Inclusive Education (Brahm Norwich, 2002) have shown a slow but steady trend towards inclusion but remarkable variation across local authorities. Such variation means that there have been many instances of children being educated in mainstream schools who, if they happened to live in another area, would be placed in a special school. In 2001, for example, a disabled pupil in Manchester was more than seven times as likely to be placed in a Special School than a child in the London borough of Newham; Manchester had 2.6 per cent of 5–15 year olds in Special Schools, whereas Newham, which has actively pursued a policy of inclusion for 18 years, had just 0.35 per cent (Norwich, 2002).

Thinking it through

To what extent do you think your school has an inclusive culture? To what extent is this culture imposed from without: Local Authority and Government and to what extent is it home grown?

Where would you place yourself on the 'Special School debate': are there certain sorts of need that you think are particularly hard to meet in a mainstream school?

Practical ways to research inclusion

As we commented at the start, researching into inclusion can be difficult because inclusion is a term which can be somewhat abstract and difficult to define and because inquiries can involve attempting to explore the feelings and convictions of others. So when you inquire into inclusion, you will need to think carefully about the methods you use for gathering evidence. What follows are some approaches that have worked in the past for those carrying out inquiries in this area.

First of all, it is very helpful if you can think through what inclusion means to you personally. Just writing your definition on a piece of paper can be very illuminating in this respect. Once you've done this, you should read a little about inclusion and particularly around how people have defined the term (we have tried to give you a start on this above). This will help prepare you for the range of attitudes that you may encounter, and as we indicated above, inform you about some of the complexities associated with inclusion. In short, reading like this will help you to know what it is you are looking for and perhaps where to look.

A near essential next step is to formulate an inquiry question. You can read more about how to do this in the Introduction. Having a question in mind will help you to decide what sort of inquiry methods are most appropriate and focus the collection of your evidence, but it's also possible to start an investigation by being more exploratory. Questionnaire surveys can be a good way to do this as they can enable you quickly to gain an overview of how a number of people think. For example, you might write a question that invites respondents to give their personal definition of inclusion: the differences here between how managers, teaching staff, non-teaching staff and pupils respond to this question can be quite illuminating. Two recent studies along exactly these lines are those by Jonathan Glazzard (2011) and Suzanne Mackenzie (2011) and you will find them both highly readable and helpful in planning your inquiry.

When you are working on an inquiry, as we have suggested above, imitation really can be the sincerest form of flattery! Part of the reason why reading academic literature is an important part of an inquiry is that articles and books contain within them accounts of how other people have inquired into the same areas that you are investigating and there is absolutely no reason why you should not replicate the methods that you read about. As you can also read in Chapter 2, it's even completely acceptable to use or adapt the questionnaires or interview questions that you find in academic texts.

You can read more about interviewing in Chapters 2 and 3, but gathering evidence in this way for inquiries about inclusion presents particular challenges. Most schools and most teachers would probably regard themselves as inclusive so direct questions, such as 'Is this an inclusive school?', are unlikely to be particularly productive. This is firstly because they are closed questions which allow a yes/no answer and secondly because they are weighted questions: responding requires the interviewee to make a political judgement about practice at their school. After all, legislation requires a school to be 'inclusive' so saying that the school or a colleague are not inclusive is in effect a quite serious criticism. Whenever you ask questions like this, there is a risk that the *validity* of what people say will be affected: put crudely, people are less likely to give you the truth if there might be implications attached to speaking that truth. It's a much better tactic to ask indirect and more open questions. These can sometimes seem bland and almost embarrassingly simple, but they are frequently a good way of getting at understandings and attitudes. So, asking 'Why is inclusion important?' or 'How can you include pupils?' can be a way of probing deeply held values as your interviewees can answer them freely without there being an obvious 'correct' answer.

Obtaining information from children can be difficult, especially since the very children whose opinions would be most valuable for an inquiry on inclusion can be those whose views are hardest to access. Pupils will, partly unconsciously, filter what they say depending on who they are speaking to, especially if that person happens to be their teacher. Also, as John Quicke (2003) points out, children aren't necessarily sophisticated analysts of their own education and in particular, they lack knowledge of alternatives with which to compare their own experiences. On the other hand, if as we've discussed, inclusion in some way revolves around the feelings of pupils then clearly there's a strong case for persisting. If possible, it's a good strategy to generate data through activities that are like normal classroom activity rather than, say, one to one interviews. So group discussions, small questionnaires or pictorial methods (for example, asking pupils to draw a spider diagram of 'things I like' and 'things I don't like' about lessons) are good techniques. Immediate, contextual questions are usually better than those that are more abstract and generalized so you might focus the question on the previous lesson or on a particular activity. For more reading on gathering evidence from pupils, we recommend Ann Lewis and Jill Porter (2007). For a large study on pupil attitudes towards inclusion, try Brahm Norwich and Narcie Kelly (2004).

There are other methods for gathering information from pupils. Observation can be an effective way of looking at social inclusion in particular. For many pupils who are marginalized and excluded, it is the out of classroom experiences that can reveal most. Observing a pupil during a break or lunchtime can provide you with real insights into their lives at school in ways that would be difficult to achieve through any sort of questioning. Similarly, don't forget the power of documents as evidence of inclusion. Pupils' work can give a vivid window onto their feelings and experiences. More directly, pupil writing can give strong evidence of pupil progress and learning especially perhaps where, for example, dyslexia, dyspraxia or dyscalculia are involved. 'Hard' school data can also tell an eloquent story; attendance data, attainment data or behaviour log data can all provide excellent supporting evidence for an inquiry into inclusion.

> ### Thinking it through
>
> What questions might you ask about inclusion at your school?
>
> Think about your 'gut feelings' about inclusion. For example, do you think that non-teaching staff share your values about inclusion? How might you gather data to support your case?
>
> Are you aware of any school policy relating to inclusion? Are you aware of any discussion about issues of inclusion within school?
>
> Think about the potential of pupils as researchers or co-researchers? What sort of projects might it be appropriate for pupils to undertake in connection with inclusion?
>
> Can you see any ethical difficulties associated with pupil research?

We end this chapter with three case studies of inquiries into inclusion that may help you to design and carry out your own study.

Case study: A pupil's view of inclusion

Guy has Special Educational Needs arising from a brain stem stroke which he suffered at the age of 5 and which resulted in him becoming quadriplegic, with the loss of his speech and language skills. Guy is now 13 years old and attends his local mainstream school. He uses a Dynavox and computer to support his educational and communication needs. Guy also indicates his responses through mouth gestures, facial expression and eye pointing. Due to the profound and multiple physical disabilities arising from his medical condition he is fully dependent upon adult support for all his self-care needs.

Guy is very interested in learning; he has good listening skills and a great interest in both factual and fictional information. His cognitive skills are considered to be unaffected by his medical condition, with at least average potential indicated. It is communication that is the major factor in Guy's difficulties. His acquisition of phonic skills is significantly delayed and, as a result, his reading skills and spelling are very limited. Guy and his parents have always expressed a preference for mainstream education and his primary school had adaptations made to facilitate this.

Together with Guy, a project was conceived that would both provide evidence for an inquiry into Guy's experiences in the school and promote his inclusion. Guy would give a presentation at a year group assembly and prepare a DVD.

'Guy's DVD' gave the school an opportunity to view inclusion from the perspective of the pupils. Planning began with Guy choosing a group of pupils to become involved in an interview that included his own questions, such as 'How does my disability affect your friendship with me?' Recording of the interview was done by Year 10 Media Studies students and led to further time filming Guy in his lessons and also in his after-school science club. He worked with a Year 10 boy to decide how to introduce and end the DVD. In addition to showing the DVD, a demonstration of Guy using his Dynavox was given at the assembly and was such a resounding success that the assembly was repeated for other year groups. His handy hints and tips continue to be discussed by pupils and staff throughout the school.

This case study both provides an example of inclusion in action and how a pupil can be involved in generating evidence about their life in school. The collaborative way in which this project has been carried out reflects both good inquiry practice in that it allowed for the gathering of meaningful data from Guy and contributed towards the inclusive ethos of the school.

Thinking it through

Can you think of pupils whose experiences might be captured in a similar way? What might the practical and ethical difficulties be in arranging such a project?

What are the weaknesses of the sort of data that has been generated here? What might such data not tell you about Guy's life?

Case study: A holistic view of inclusion

Harry is the Special Educational Needs Coordinator (SENCo) and Year 4 teacher in a primary school in inner-city Bradford which has about 450 children, 41 per cent of whom are on the school's Special Educational Needs (SEN) register. Harry wanted to carry out a critical analysis of the provision that the school had made for Saif, a Year 5 pupil recently diagnosed with autism, looking at how that provision is impacting on his progress both academically and socially?

Thinking it through

What data currently available in school and held by other professionals might be helpful to undertake a study of this kind?

How might undertaking this inquiry improve Harry's own knowledge of supporting pupils with specific learning difficulties?

Harry learnt more about autism using general websites such as that of the National Autistic Society (www.autism.org.uk) and the Autism Education Trust (www.autismeducatiotrust.org.uk). He then used the *British Journal of Special Education* to identify some of the key issues surrounding educational provision for children with Special Educational Needs.

Harry wanted to work with a pupil, Saif, who wasn't in his own class. He therefore had to explain the purpose of his enquiry to the teachers, teaching assistants and other professionals who worked with Saif and get their agreement to support his inquiry. As this was part of his SENCo duties, Harry did not need to get any ethical clearance from his university but he did check this with his tutor prior to beginning the study.

The first task that Harry needed to do was to collect all that data that was already held about Saif, this included:

- end of year reports;
- Saif's Individual Education Plan;
- Saif's work, including assessed pieces of work.

Harry looked at all these documents searching for evidence of progress in academic or social terms over a school year and to help him describe the provision that was in place to support the pupil. When he wrote up his inquiry later he would be able to use extracts from these documents to support the claims he made in his account.

The documents could only provide part of the story. In order to form a more complete picture, Harry observed Saif in small group work, away from the classroom and in social situations such as playtime and dinner. Before each session he thought carefully about the focus of the observation and how he would record what he had seen. For example, to observe playtime, Harry designed a record sheet that logged and described the interactions Saif had, with whom and for how long.

Pulling all this evidence and reading together, Harry was able to present a holistic evaluation of how the school were including Saif taking into account both academic and social dimensions and offering suggestions for developing and improving practice for pupils like Saif in future.

Case study: An 'Every Child Matters' approach

Sue based her inquiry on Neville, a Year 2 pupil. Her inquiry question was quite specific: how is Neville included in school life with respect to the Every Child Matters outcomes (be healthy, stay safe, enjoy and achieve, make a positive contribution and achieve economic well-being)?

Sue collected evidence about Neville's academic progress. School data showed that Neville was working below level 1 in reading, writing and maths. Neville struggled to access the curriculum as his reading and writing skills were well below the age expected levels. With regard to the 'achieve' aspect of the Every Child Matters policy it was clear then that Neville was not making good progress.

When she presented her inquiry, Sue was able to include work from reading, writing and maths to display the progress that Neville had made in these areas. At the time of the inquiry, Neville had one-to-one reading sessions and phonics twice a week, strong differentiation and teaching assistant support in class. Speaking to a number of adults who work with Neville helped Sue form the judgement that current provision was not meeting Neville's needs well and was also taking teacher and teaching assistant time away from other children in the class.

With regard to the 'be healthy' aspect of ECM, Sue spoke to the school SENCo and found that the school had a Child Protection file on Neville which documented issues, some of which were linked to his health including cleanliness. In line with this, staff had raised many concerns surrounded Neville's safety and home life. Sue asked permission to read Neville's Individual Education Plan to see what Neville had contributed to the last review.

Speaking to Neville's class teacher, Sue learnt that Neville did not take part in any extra-curricular clubs and at lunch times often stayed by himself or with one particular child. He found communicating with both his peers and adults difficult and he was often said to be withdrawn and 'in a world of his own'. When, together with the SENCo, Sue informally interviewed Neville, this assessment was confirmed. School data showed that Neville had average attendance for his school: 92 per cent in Reception and 97 per cent in Year 1, but since the start of Year 2, Neville's attendance had dropped dramatically to 67 per cent.

Thinking it through

Sue collected a wide range of data for her case study, what are the implications of this a) for the validity (see Chapter 2) of the inquiry; b) for the timescale of the inquiry; c) for Sue's workload. What do you think about the amount of evidence that Sue has generated here?

Sue dealt with some quite sensitive information in this inquiry. What ethical precautions do you think she would have had to take when carrying out her investigation?

How and with whom do you think Sue might share the findings of this inquiry?

Bringing it together

- Inclusion lies somewhere in the balance between principles, practicalities and what legislation requires. Inquiring into inclusion requires some appreciation of all three.
- A survey of colleagues, asking 'What does inclusion mean?', or of pupils, asking 'When do you feel included?', is a simple and productive way to start an inclusion inquiry.
- Inclusion is a challenging but rewarding area to investigate in which the feelings and perceptions of pupils can be important evidence. Getting that evidence can be problematic.
- Among the particular suggested techniques for inquiring into inclusion are: using 'normal' classroom activities, observing pupils out of lessons, looking at pupil work or asking them to express their feelings through drawing.

References

Ainscow, M. (2007) Taking an inclusive turn. *Journal of Research in Special Educational Needs.* Vol. 7, No. 1, pp. 3–7.

Bercow, J. (2008) *The Bercow Report. A Review of Services for Children and Young People (0–19) with Speech, Language and Communication Needs.* DCSF-00632-2008. Available at http://www.education. gov.uk/publications/eOrderingDownload/Bercow-Report.pdf (Accessed 27-Aug-11).

Booth, T. and Ainscow, M. (2011) *Index for Inclusion: Developing Learning and Participation in Schools (3rd edition)*. Centre for Studies in Inclusive Education.

Centre for Studies on Inclusive Education (2004) *Ten Reasons for Inclusion*, Bristol: CSIE.

DfEE (1997) Excellence for all children. London: HMSO.

DfE (2011) *Green Paper: Children and Young People with Special Educational Needs and Disabilities – Call for Views*. Available at http://www.education.gov.uk/consultations/ (Accessed 24-Aug-11).

DfE (2010) *The Importance of Teaching – the Schools White Paper*. Available at http://www.education.gov.uk/publications/standard/publicationDetail/Page1/CM%207980 (Accessed 24-Aug-11).

DfES (2001) *Special Educational Needs Code of Practice*. London: HMSO.

DfES publications (2004) *Removing Barriers to Achievement, The Government's Strategy for SEN*. London: HMSO.

Frederickson, N. and Cline, T. (2009) *Special Educational Needs, Inclusion and Diversity*. Maidenhead: Open University Press.

Glazzard, J. (2011) Perceptions of the barriers to effective inclusion in one primary school: voices of teachers and teaching assistants. *Support for Learning*, Vol. 26, No. 2, pp. 56–63.

Hart, S., Drummond, M. and McIntyre, D. (2007) Learning without limits, in: L. Florian (Ed.) *The Sage Handbook of Special Education*. London: Sage.

Lamb, B. (2009) *Lamb Inquiry: Special Educational Needs and Parental Confidence*. DCSF. Available at http://www.dcsf.gov.uk/lambinquiry/downloads/8553-lamb-inquiry.pdf (Accessed 27-Aug-11).

Lewis, A. and Porter, J. (2007) Research and pupil voice. in *The Sage Handbook of Special Education*. London: Sage.

Lindsay, G. (2003) Inclusive education: a critical perspective. *British Journal of Special Education*, Vol. 30, No. 1, pp. 3–12.

Mackenzie, S. (2011) Yes, but . . .': rhetoric, reality and resistance in teaching assistants' experiences of inclusive education. *Support for Learning*, Vol. 26, No. 2, pp. 64–71.

Meyer, L. H., Minondo, S., Fisher, S. Larsen, M. J., Dunmore, S., Black, J. W. and D'Aquanni, M. (1998) Frames of friendship: Social relationships of adolescents with diverse abilities. In Meyer, L. H., Park, H. S., Grenot-Scheyer, M., Schwarz, I. S. and Harry, B. (eds.) *Making Friends. The Influence of Culture and Development*. Baltimore: Paul H Brookes.

Norwich, B. (2002) Education, inclusion and individual differences: recognizing and resolving dilemmas. *British Journal of Educational Studies*, Vol. 50, No. 4, pp. 482–502.

Norwich, B. and Kelly, N. (2004) Pupils' views on inclusion: moderate learning difficulties and bullying in mainstream and special schools. *British Educational Research Journal*, Vol. 30, No. 1, pp. 43–65.

Ofsted (2010) *The Special Educational Needs and Disability Review: A Statement is not Enough*. London: HMSO.

Quicke, J. (2003) Educating the pupil voice. *Support for Learning*, Vol. 18, No. 2, pp. 51–7.

Reynolds, M. (1989) An historical perspective: the delivery of special education to mildly disabled and at-risk students. *Remedial and Special Education*, Vol. 10, No. 6, pp. 7–11.

Rieser, R. and Mason, M. (1992) *Disability Equality in the Classroom: A Human Rights Issue*. London: Disability Equality in Education.

Salt Review (2010) Supply of teachers for pupils with severe and complex learning difficulties. London: HMSO.

UNESCO (1994) *The Salamanca Statement and Framework for Action on Special Needs Education*. Paris: UNESCO.

8 Inquiring into Collaborative Working

Brendan Higgins and Erica Mace

Introduction

Understanding someone else's perspective is often difficult. When one person is a teacher (*a professional*) and the other a parent (*a non-professional*), different experiences, expectations, priorities and pressures shape their relationship. When educationalists work alongside others, for example, health or social care professionals on child-centred issues, different perspectives are almost inevitable. These pose obvious challenges for successful interaction. Moving their dialogue from understanding through to partnership and ultimately collaboration is a significant journey. Even between professionals within one institution, the development of successful collaboration is often taken for granted. This chapter is about inquiring into how effective partnerships are achieved, the benefits they bring and the impact they create.

The drive to improve the quality of schools at all levels continues to be a priority of government policy. Over the past 30 years many collaborative arrangements have been encouraged to lead to better outcomes for *all* pupils. Increasingly the expectation that collaboration can be structured to support leadership, development and change is evidenced by the Every Child Matters agenda (ECM) and school workforce reforms. The nature and scope of collaboration is vast. It ranges from small-scale teamwork within one school to partnerships between schools and beyond, involving a range of external agencies. The aspiration for teaching to become a masters' level profession is in itself an imaginative collaborative development between schools and universities for the professional development of teachers.

Thinking it through

In the light of this context, think about the range of collaborations you are currently involved in. How informal or structured are they presently? How effective are they in meeting their objectives?

Which collaborations are directly focused on improving pupil welfare, development and achievement and which are more focused on the partnership structures?

In this chapter collaboration in different contexts is explored. A focus on how the children's workforce is changing is used to review benefits and challenges of working with support staff within the classroom and school. The importance of including parents and a range of other agencies in collaborations is examined. Recognizing the huge impact school has on children's lives is essential for any teacher. As a masters student or as a practitioner inquiring as part of your professional development, the ability to reflect on and critically analyse evidence about this collaborative impact is central. As such, it should contribute to your development as a reflective practitioner and enhance your participation and effectiveness in any collegiate and collaborative learning community.

The suggestions for reading and the literature review on working with colleagues we present here are designed to help you think about some of the key issues underpinning effective collaborative practice and how these may be evaluated in improving pupil learning. Research evidence to support the use of collaboration and the implications for future developments is considered. Two case studies, one from Key Stage 2, focusing on working with teaching assistants, and one from Key Stage 3, on a curriculum project for vulnerable and challenging pupils involving parents and external agencies, are presented to examine issues of collaboration. These provide possible ways for you to explore and develop inquiry into collaborative practice within your own classroom, school and with other partners and agencies.

You will see in what follows that we make several references to Every Child Matters (ECM). We are aware at the time of writing that ECM is likely to be replaced as a Government policy focus but we continue to use the term here because it describes a set of desirable outcomes for children which we feel will continue to define collaborative working whatever terminology is adopted and because there is a corpus of literature around ECM that is particularly valuable for those inquiring in this area.

Reading about collaborative practice: Developing inquiry ideas

The key to searching for relevant reading in this area is to be clear about your focus in each particular area. For example, if you are interested in the Every Child Matters agenda, you may wish to understand this policy from a philosophical angle in the first instance. Julian Stern (2007) attempts to unpick the policy framework, asking, what does it mean to *matter*, given that we all understand that every child does matter? His review usefully develops a philosophical perspective on this question while linking such thinking to empirical research evidence from work with children aged 6–11. The notion and nature of the school and wider community is explored to determine the commonly held values, beliefs and practices that express how teachers, other staff and parents work in relationships *because the children matter*.

Alternatively, your focus may be an overarching consideration of issues and challenges related to the development and introduction of ECM. In other words, how do we make ECM happen effectively? Alma Harris and Tracey Allen (2009) propose that there are four key processes associated with successful implementation of ECM:

- energizing and orientating the culture of the school towards ECM through the prioritization by leaders and managers
- establishing and consolidating links with partners, creating a shared vision or purpose;
- developing community-wide support especially with parents
- securing external support from local authorities, businesses and other agencies to fund extended services and new initiatives.

You may wish to develop an inquiry by selecting one of these areas or choose a narrower focus related to your school context.

Teachers committed to ECM are determined to improve pupil well-being and increase achievement. They recognize the need to develop effective collaboration between school and parents and carers. This partnership is of paramount importance given that home and school are the two key settings in children's lives. Leon Feinstein et al. (2008), attempt to understand the detrimental impact of social disadvantage on pupils which is often related to their parents' abilities to take advantage of educational opportunities. You may wish to explore through inquiry opportunities to improve parental involvement. Alternatively, rather than focusing on the parent-teacher perspective your inquiry might examine how children operate within and view such partnerships (Rosalind Edwards, 2002).

Whatever your main focus, you will need to extend your literature search across academic journals to help to illuminate the particulars of your own context. For example, the concept of 'hard to reach parents' is one familiar to schools, especially those in challenging circumstances and is often cited as a reason for difficulties. Jill Crozier and Jane Davies (2007) challenge this view and suggest that it may be the school that creates the barriers or inhibition to parental contact. Their study focuses on home-school relations with particular reference to Bangladeshi and Pakistani parents. It raises interesting cultural and community specific issues that may be of relevance in your own context.

In addition to the academic literature, there are professional, government and other agency publications that are useful in examining collaboration, workforce reform and ECM, for example, the Specialist Schools and Academies Trust (www.ssat.org.uk) or National College for School Leadership (www.nationalcollege.org.uk). In one NCSL publication, Cottrell (2009) investigates the workforce reform from a historical perspective and as a policy framework before examining the educational impact it has made.

His research uses a case study approach, and the aims, methodology and findings are clearly presented as one possible approach to inquiry for your consideration.

Research Reports (RR) commissioned by the Department for Children, Schools and Families (DCSF) are very useful sources of information. DCSF, RR005 and DCSF, RR027 critically review the deployment and impact of support staff following the workforce reform agenda (see Peter Blatchford et al., 2007, 2008). An excellent study of the involvement of parents and carers in children's education is given in DCSF, RR034 (Mark Peters et al., 2008). There are several ways to utilize such literature. First, *executive summaries* in the reports provide the reader with a clear focused overview of the key issues. Rich and detailed data is gathered from a variety of research methods and presented in a range of formats. These may assist the inquiring teacher, guiding them to possible methodologies and ways to present data findings applicable on a smaller scale in the classroom or school.

Ofsted, the Office for Standards in Education, Children's Services and Skills regulates and inspects the care and education of children and young people (www.ofsted.gov.uk). The agency provides a substantial range of data to support inquiry into collaborative practice. Hundreds of inspections and visits take place each week, listening to the views of service users and providers, publishing findings within Inspection reports on their website. In addition, themed and subject-specific findings and recommendations on wider issues within the care, learning and skills agenda, as well as statistical information, can be found in their publications and research area. An overview of findings is given in the Ofsted annual reports.

Interrogating these various resources is worth considering. A search, using the Ofsted Annual Report (2009/10), available online, reveals that *parents* (and carers), are mentioned over 100 times, whereas support staff and workforce are mentioned on fewer than ten occasions. Is this significant? Certainly the analysis of parental views expressed for Ofsted reports provides important data. You may use the Ofsted summary of inspection reports listing 'outstanding' practice to carry out a comparative review of schools in similar phases and localities. Benchmarking in this way is helpful in guiding you to identify and analyse best practice in collaborations, partnerships and involvement of parents. More importantly it promotes your critical evaluation of your own situation in comparison to others.

Thinking it through

What are the ethical issues you need to consider in an inquiry into collaborative working? What do you need to do to ensure that it is:

(a) sensitively handled?
(b) protects confidentiality and anonymity?
(c) enhances and supports rather than undermines existing relationships?

Collaborative working – the end of 'The Lonely Profession'?

This section is in the form of an exemplar literature review covering workforce reform and the role of other staff working alongside and supporting teachers. It examines research evidence for the impact and effectiveness of such arrangements and relates to the case study that follows.

Additional adults such as teaching assistants (TAs) have become a feature of mainstream primary classrooms in recent years, marking the end of 'The Lonely Profession'. The increase in numbers of TAs stems largely from the move towards inclusion following the Warnock Report (DES, 1978), which stressed that, if at all possible, children should be educated within mainstream schools, with additional adult support where necessary.

Following the Education Act and the Special Educational Needs and Disability Act 2001, large numbers of additional adults were appointed to support SEN pupils in mainstream schools. The government's remodelling of the school workforce has enabled many TAs to extend their roles, thus developing their skills and careers.

The trend towards parental involvement which began in the early 1980s has resulted in many parents volunteering to work in classrooms on a regular basis. Volunteers from the local community are often welcomed in schools and colleges to hear readers and help with special projects. Students and those on work experience may also appear, offering their time and talents. Nursery nurses, speech and language therapists, learning mentors, occupational therapists and educational psychologists may also become involved.

However, it seems that having other adults involved in the classroom does not automatically lead to improvement:

> There seems to have been the assumption that these people would effortlessly and seamlessly slide into the classroom to work alongside the class teacher; that simply to provide 'help' for the teacher would automatically be a Good Thing. Unfortunately it isn't; often it can be a burden rather than a help.
>
> (Thomas, 1992, xi)

The incorporation of additional adults into the classroom 'mix' needs careful management in terms of training, definition of roles and responsibilities and the provision of opportunities for communication of information and ideas.

How can teaching assistants contribute to long-term benefits for children?

Two of the many ways in which the involvement of teaching assistants (TAs) can benefit children include raising self-esteem and promoting learning and achievement.

Raising children's self-esteem

Before children can begin to learn, they need to feel settled and positive about themselves and their learning environment. Adults assisting children are well placed to relieve anxiety which may prevent learning taking place, for example, they can encourage a child who is inclined to panic when faced with mathematics tasks.

Adults can also encourage children by praising their effort and progress. Thomas Good and Jere Brophy (1977), cited in Jean Gross (1996), found that when teachers increased their use of praise, the behaviour and performance of a low achieving group improved dramatically.

TAs have much to offer in terms of the pastoral care of pupils. Gavin Reid (2003) notes that TAs who have received training can help children through counselling and that a combination of counselling and academic intervention is more effective than intervention alone. TAs are often able to form emotional bonds with children which are increasingly important in communities where parent-child relationships are poor. Pupils may find access to a TA easier than to a teacher; in some cases, a pupil may even relate better to the TA (Anne Moran and Lesley Abbott, 2002).

Teacher stress and workload can be relieved by having TAs in the classroom; this in turn will positively affect the children's experience. Graham Butt and Ann Lance (2005) report that 80 per cent of primary teachers agreed that working with TAs reduced their workload.

TAs have an important role in promoting inclusion by modelling socially acceptable behaviour and encouraging healthy social attitudes. Peter Farrell (1997) notes they may do this by helping children to resolve disputes through discussion and negotiation. Finally, TAs can play a vital role in caring for the medical needs of pupils. Without this vital support, the inclusion of many pupils with special medical needs would not be possible.

Promoting learning and achievement

Surprisingly, there is research evidence to suggest that the introduction of additional adults does not automatically guarantee the raising of pupils' attainment. Peter Blatchford et al. found:

> . . . no clear effects of additional staff and adults on children's educational progress in any of the three years of KS1. (Blatchford et al., 2002, 5)

Crucially, though, Blatchford et al. make the point that the adult help varied in its effectiveness and they concluded this was probably the main reason why clear evidence of benefits to children's progress was not present. A study by Julian Elliott et al. (2000) likewise reported a lack of progress in reading skills following an intervention programme delivered by volunteer support. Elliot et al. concluded that adult helpers need to have a close working relationship with the class teacher who may offer guidance and feedback on the assistant's work.

The need for appropriate training for those working in the classroom is a recurrent theme in the literature. Ofsted (2005) found that the presence of TAs can improve the quality of teaching, particularly where TAs work in close partnership with a teacher, following a clearly laid out intervention programme for which they have been trained. Intervention studies which have successfully employed TAs or other adults who have been specially trained include those by

Janice Ryder et al. (2008). Nancy Scammacca et al. (2007) found that the effect sizes of interventions provided by non-teachers were similar to those delivered by teachers, while Sharon Vaughn and Greg Roberts (2007) concluded that highly-structured and well-planned interventions delivered by TAs tended to result in improved outcomes for students. The key to successful intervention, therefore, appears to be *the way in which adult support is used.*

There is ongoing debate as to whether TAs should withdraw individuals and small groups from the classroom in order to provide additional help. Some feel withdrawal promotes exclusion and draws attention to the fact that those children are 'different'. Richard Rose (2000, 195) quotes Gary Thomas et al. (1998), who suggest withdrawal may adversely affect pupils' self-esteem. This, however, must be balanced by the advantages of relocating pupils to a quieter setting with fewer distractions which may be more conducive to concentration, the need for which is often an issue for children with SEN.

Case study: TA – delivered intervention to meet the needs of primary school children with literacy difficulties

Background

Prior to the introduction of a TA-delivered intervention, a school had bought in the services of a Specialist Support Teacher (SST) for one day per week to assess children with Special Educational Needs (SEN) in literacy and to teach small groups of children from each class to improve their literacy skills.

The advantage of this method of working was that the children were taught by a Specialist SEN Teacher. However, the time given to each group was approximately 20 minutes per week and because there were few opportunities for professional discussion, there was minimal overlap between what was being delivered to the group and the support which the children were receiving in class.

Organization of the TA intervention groups

It was decided that the role of the SST would change. The SST would produce planning for intervention groups to be taken by TAs in two, 30 minute sessions per week. This would enable the expertise of the SST to be passed on to the TAs, while allowing the children to receive more support. The SST assessed the children's phonic knowledge, high frequency word reading and spelling and their reading and spelling ages. Individual specific, measurable, achievable, realistic and time-related (SMART) targets were then set for each child.

Nine intervention groups were set up according to the children's Individual Education Plan (IEP) targets, each group consisting of approximately six children from mixed year groups who would be working on similar targets. The groups were taken by TAs who worked in the same Key Stage as the children, although there was some overlap.

The IEP targets formed the learning objectives for the group. The SST planned material for the TAs to deliver: each session typically consisting of a visual or auditory memory game, followed by multisensory activities designed to develop the children's alphabetic/phonic knowledge, reading and spelling strategies and rhyming skills.

Resources were ordered on the advice of the SST and the TAs received training in how to use them. The TAs were asked to complete the weekly planning sheets and return them to the SST so that the following week's planning could take their comments and observations regarding the children's progress into account. *This was the main opportunity for conversation, although informal discussion also took place before and after school and in the staff room during break times.* Termly meetings were held between TAs, SST and Special Needs Co-ordinator (SENCo) to allow for discussion and to introduce new activities and resources.

It was made clear that the SST's planning should not be restrictive; once TAs were familiar with the needs of the children and the resources and activities, they were encouraged to bring their own creativity to the group sessions, providing the learning objectives were being met. Some TAs embraced this opportunity by developing their own games and resources. The TAs were also trained to assess the children's progress each term. All reported that they were encouraged by the effect their work had on the children's progress, which contributed to their job satisfaction.

Because of their constant presence in the school, the TAs were able to monitor the extent to which the children's work in the intervention groups was contributing to their progress in the classroom. They were also in a position to be able to note any improvements in the pupils' self-esteem.

Regularity and quality of feedback were vital factors in the success of the intervention. On a few occasions, where feedback sheets were not returned by TAs or not completed in such a way as to inform future planning, the process was less effective.

The most effective intervention arose when planning sheets were handed in weekly with specific comments relating to individual children's progress or suggested areas for development. For example, comments such as 'Bobby is still getting mixed up between j and g and u and y', or 'The group needs more practice on looking for words within words' were much more helpful than general comments such as, 'The group enjoyed the game.' Specific feedback meant the subsequent week's planning could be targeted to meet particular group or individual needs.

The role of the Specialist Support Teacher

The change in role of the SST from teaching groups throughout the day to planning for TAs to deliver group work enabled a far wider support service to be made available to the school.

The SST spent an hour and a half each week looking over the TAs' evaluated planning from the previous week and producing a new planning sheet for each TA. Termly assessments and IEP reviews led to the setting of new targets which were used to update the groups' learning objectives.

The remainder of the SST's time was spent carrying out in-depth assessments of pupils' literacy and numeracy needs, writing reports, observing children's learning in the classroom and otherwise supporting the role of the SENCo.

At the end of the academic year, the children's progress in phonic knowledge, high frequency words and their reading and spelling ages were assessed by the SST.

Comparing the efficacy of the two approaches

Clearly the impact on pupil progress is at the heart of this collaborative work. To assess which system had given rise to greater pupil progress, data from previous years could be compared with that from the current intervention programme. *Would children make more progress attending one session per week delivered by a SST or through two weekly sessions planned by the SST and delivered by TAs?*

Thinking it through

How would you develop an inquiry to further evaluate TA effectiveness in this case study?

What are the benefits and challenges in using TA interviews, analysis of their reporting sheets, pupil voice, direct observations or video recording of the sessions?

Is this model of collaboration possible between teacher and cover supervisor or other support staff in the school setting?

External agencies and parents

The use of an alternative curriculum to meet the needs of challenging or vulnerable pupils is common practice in schools. However, it often requires external partners to be involved and supportive in encouraging the possibilities. Sometimes pupils, parents and school staff accept the convenience and rationale for such arrangements without appreciating the implications or assessing the benefit. On the other hand, imaginative and engaging activities may be dismissed and undermined by staff, parents or pupils who do not wish to engage in what is perceived as a 'lesser' curriculum.

Case study: Small groups as a way of developing pupils' social skills

Context

A small secondary school was experiencing significant issues of disengagement by a number of KS3 pupils. A profile of these pupils revealed low levels of prior attainment at KS2 and socially challenging and disadvantaged home backgrounds. The problems manifested themselves in very poor attendance, or even non-attendance, behaviour problems (disruptive, hyperactive or withdrawn non-communicative), and in a few cases, Child Protection concerns. Pupils often demonstrated low self esteem and were vulnerable to bullying or were themselves bullies. Educational Welfare Support officers (EWSs) were already involved with these pupils, primarily focused on improving attendance.

However, the nature of the pupils' problems required support and intervention from other agencies such as Educational Psychology, Social Services and the Youth Offending team. Parents were often in conflict with school and these agencies since their contact was frequently associated with negative meetings around behaviour or poor attendance.

Conversation with Colleagues

This complex scenario poses many problems but in essence three key issues arise:

What can be done?

How can the school develop a coherent partnership with a range of agencies and individuals to address the problem?

Whatever the proposed solution, how could it be evaluated to identify what makes it work?

Inquiry proposal

The Head of Key Stage 3 proposed that a focused separate curriculum project was required to engage pupils. The aim was to develop social skills and self-esteem in the pupils through a small group setting. Technology, art and music using 'making' and 'creative' activity themes would be provided. Funding for some staffing and resources was needed. The EWS service, determined to improve attendance and develop more access to the pupils and parents, was willing to pay for a TA for two afternoons. The school had links with a local youth club and they were happy to be involved using their premises and additional staff to assist with the project activities. The Head of KS3 liaised with the EWS and youth club proposing that up to ten pupils in each of Y7 and Y8 would be selected to attend for one afternoon over a period of eight weeks.

The school's initial task was to invite parents to individual meetings to explain the aims of the project and seek their support. The afternoon session was designed to be extended to 5.30 pm or beyond into the normal youth club opening times. This would facilitate more opportunity to develop contact with the pupils. More importantly, their parents would be invited in on a regular basis to observe their son or daughter and to have meetings with staff from school, the club or other supporting agencies. Where attendance was the primary issue, EWSs would meet parents to discuss actions. If another social or health-related problem was evident, social services, the school nurse or other appropriate support worker could be engaged. The idea of this arrangement was to make the meeting of parents and professionals more informal while preserving confidentiality and sensitivity. Holding the meeting at a venue other than the school was perceived as less threatening. By removing negative connotations it provided an opportunity for parents to see their child in enjoyable, productive activities making progress.

The Head of KS3 acted as coordinator, assisted by a school TA. The TA would accompany the pupils to the club and stay with them to assist in activities. Youth workers from the club liaised with the Head of KS3 to set up the various 'making' or 'creative' activities. These included, preparing food, photography, video, pottery, other art work and percussion sessions. The school's non-teaching Pastoral Manager liaised with parents and the professionals from the various agencies to set up appropriate meetings during the extended afternoon sessions.

Thinking it through

How would you frame interviews for the different partners in this collaboration to explore, for example, their understanding, roles and responsibilities and effectiveness? What other data could be collected for such an inquiry?

How would you approach observations and interviews with parents and pupils? What other data collection would you make to support findings from such interviews?

Classroom videoing of lessons in school was undertaken by the Head of KS3 as part of the school's normal observation procedures prior to the start of the project. This included videoing pupils on the project. Recording their engagement and behaviour in school provided a baseline starting point for future comparisons. The youth club video-recorded activities of pupil involvement and achievement for sharing with parents. This enabled school staff to analyse and evaluate pupil progress and engagement and compare with each pupil's attitude in school, before, during and after the project. In addition, the club asked the pupils to record video diaries on their involvement with the activities and personal comments about their feelings of confidence, commitment, being part of a team and so on.

Thinking it through

One advantage of video-recording is the detailed primary evidence gathered which may be reviewed many times. But how do you ensure it does not have an adverse effect on pupils? What are the ethical issues you need to think about when making recordings and video diaries?

The case study could promote inquiries to focus on:

- pupils and their engagement, attendance and change of behaviour
- parents and their understanding of the issues
- different professionals working collaboratively
- communication underpinning effective partnership, leadership strategies.

Drawing it together

Collaborative working is an integral and increasingly important aspect of work in all schools at every level. The processes underpinning effective collaboration are complex and sensitive. They rely upon constant communication, flexibility and adaptability to change including a strong commitment from leaders and managers. However, the key ingredient is clarifying a shared understanding of the agreed aims and purpose focused on the pupils' welfare and achievement.

The two case studies highlight important issues from different perspectives. In the first case study, potential benefits from the *workforce reform* were examined where a teacher and TA constructed effective and efficient interventions to address pupil literacy. A comprehensive literature review examined the research evidence around TA and teacher collaboration. The second case study, a multi-agency approach, explored ways to improve *inclusion* for disadvantaged and disengaged pupils. Primarily aimed at the ECM agenda, it sought to improve and increase *parental involvement*. This included consideration of the sensitive, ethical and practical issues of video observation.

In many senses, success in life depends upon knowing how to get along with people. Relationships are important and we need to understand and develop them. They are at the core of our educational endeavours. Effective collaborative practice, however, requires more. Where relationships are weak, strained or broken, professional expertise and commitment of teachers and all other partners needs to be planned, resourced, led and managed to clarify purpose, set achievable agendas and evaluate outcomes. Of course, *every child matters;* and in all successful educational collaborations, *every teacher, every support staff individual, every parent and every other partner matters.*

References

Argent, K. (2007) *Every Child Matters:* change for parents/carers and families? Can schools work with families to promote knowledge and understanding of government expectations? *Education 3–13,* Vol. 35, No. 3, 295–303.

Blatchford, P., Martin, C., Moriarty V., Bassett, P. and Goldstein, H. (2002) *'Pupil Adult Ratio Differences and Educational Progress over Reception and Key Stage 1'* DfES RR 335. London: HMSO.

Blatchford, P., Bassett, P., Brown, P., Martin, C., Russell, A. and Webster, R. (2007). *Deployment and Impact of Support Staff in Schools: Report on Findings from the Second National Questionnaire Survey of Schools, Support Staff and Teachers (strand 1, wave 2 - 2006) – Research Report RR005.* Nottingham: Department for Children Schools and Families.

Blatchford, P., Bassett, P., Brown, P., Martin, C., Russell, A. and Webster, R. (2008) *Deployment and Impact of Support Staff in Schools and the Impact of the National Agreement: Results from Strand 2 Wave 1 - 2005/06 Research Report RR027.* Nottingham: Department for Children Schools and Families.

Butt, G. and Lance, A. (2005) Modernizing the roles of support staff in primary schools: changing focus, changing function. *Educational Review,* Vol. 57, No. 2, pp. 39–49.

Cottrell, M. (2009) The impact of workforce reforms. *Research Associate Report* (NCSL).

Crozier, G. and Davies, J. (2007) Hard to reach parents or hard to reach schools? A discussion of home-school relations, with particular reference to Bangladeshi and Pakistani parents. *British Educational Research Journal,* Vol. 33, No. 3, pp. 295–313.

DES (1978) The Warnock Report: Special Educational Needs Report of the Committee of Enquiry into the Education of Handicapped Children and Young People. London: HMSO.

Edwards, R., Ed. (2002). *Children, Home and School: Regulation, Autonomy or Connection? Future of Childhood Series.* London: Routledge Falmer.

Elliott, J., Arthurs, J. and Williams, R. (2000) Volunteer support in the primary classroom: the long-term impact of one initiative upon children's reading performance. *British Educational Research Journal,* Vol. 26, No. 2, pp. 227–44.

Farrell, P. (1997) The integration of children with severe learning difficulties: a review of the recent literature. *Journal of Applied Research in Intellectual Disabilities,* Vol. 10, No. 1, pp. 1–14.

Feinstein, L., Duckworth, K. and Sabates, R. (2008). *Education and the Family: Passing Success Across the Generations.* London: Routledge.

Good, T. and Brophy, J. (1977) *Looking in Classrooms.* Boston: Pearson/Allyn and Bacon.

Gross, J. (1996) *Special Educational Needs In The Primary School.* Buckingham: Open University Press.

Harris, A. and Allen, T. (2009) Ensuring every child matters: issues and implications for school leadership. *School Leadership and Management,* Vol. 29, No. 4, pp. 337–52.

Moran, A. and Abbott, L. (2002) Developing inclusive schools: the pivotal role of teaching assistants in promoting inclusion in special and mainstream schools in Northern Ireland. *European Journal of Special Needs Education,* Vol. 17, No. 2, pp. 161–73.

Ofsted (2005) *Remodelling the School Workforce.* London: HMSO.

Ofsted (2010) *The Annual Report of Her Majesty's Chief Inspector of Education, Children's Services and Skills 2009/10*, Ofsted. Available online at: www.ofsted.gov.uk/publications/annualreport0910 (Accessed 10-Jun-11).

Peters, M., Seeds, K., Goldstein, A. and Coleman, N. (2008*). Parental Involvement in Children's Education 2007 – Research Report RR034*. Nottingham: Department for Children Schools and Families.

Reid, G. (2003) *Dyslexia: A Practitioner's Handbook.* London: Wiley.

Rose, R. (2000) 'Using classroom support in a primary school – A single school case study' *British Journal of Special Education,* Vol. 27, No. 4, pp. 191–6.

Ryder, J.F., Tumner, W.E. and Greaney, K.T. (2008) Explicit instruction in phonemic awareness and phonologically-based decoding skills as an intervention strategy for struggling readers in whole language classrooms. *Reading and Writing,* Vol. 21, pp. 349–69.

Scammacca, N., Vaughn, S., Roberts, G., Wanzek, J. and Torgeson, J.K. (2007) *Extensive Reading Interventions in Grade K-3: From Research to Practice.* Portsmouth NH: RMC Research Corporation, Center on Instruction.

Stern, J. (2007) Mattering: what it means to matter in school. *Education 3–13,* Vol. 35, No. 3, pp. 283–93.

Thomas, G. (1992) *Effective Classroom Teamwork – Support or Intrusion?* London: Routledge.

Thomas, G., Walker. D. and Webb, J. (1998). The making of the Inclusive School. London: Routledge Falmer.

Vaughn, S. and Roberts, G. (2007) Secondary interventions in reading: Providing additional instruction for students at risk. *Teaching Exceptional Children,* Vol. 39, pp. 40–6.

Inquiring into Leadership and Management 9

Ian Price and Nick Mitchell

Chapter Outline

Introduction

Writers always have to make guesses about their readers. We imagine that several of you reading this chapter now will be studying a leadership and management course or module and are looking for some guidance, perhaps even some inspiration to help you. It's hard enough for teachers to lead and manage; after all we were all trained as teachers, not as managers: inquiring into how we and others do this is difficult for a number of reasons which we'll explore in this chapter. Unfortunately, our experience is that many leadership and management courses do little to help teachers genuinely inquire into practice and as a result many teachers emerge from these courses without having their practice or the practice of others challenged or changed. The philosophy of this book and of this chapter is that good inquiry in the classroom has the potential to transform what you see, what you think and what you do. We believe that this is true, if not truer for leadership and management than for any of the other areas covered in this book.

This chapter aims to help you inquire into leadership and management in your organization and beyond, putting your own leadership in the picture. We start by outlining the distinction between leadership and management and why understanding this is important. Then we explore something of the context within which school leaders and managers operate today: in doing so we shall be pointing to some potential areas for inquiries. Next the chapter invites you to think more personally about yourself as an inquirer and as a leader. Finally we will look at some ideas from the work of others that might be able to apply to your inquiry and your practice; we will also briefly consider we might learn from existing research in this area.

Leadership and management

To inquire into leadership and management it is necessary to understand the difference between the two. *Leadership* in educational contexts and in general can be seen as a strategic activity in which the leader seeks to influence those around her. It can involve holding and transmitting strong personal values and 'visions' and influencing the motivations and actions of others. You'll also read the term *distributed leadership*, which usually means a sort of collective leadership involving delegation and empowerment of colleagues although as you'd imagine, the extent to which power is genuinely distributed in such arrangements varies. There is a good review of the literature on distributed leadership by Nigel Bennett et al. (2003).

Management activities, on the other hand, are likely to be more concerned with the efficient running of existing organizational structures. It's perhaps likely that you'll imagine at the start that inquiring into management is more straightforward and in some ways, you might be right. However, once you start reading what some authors have written on leadership and management (we would recommend the book by Tony Bush and David Middlewood (2005) as a starter here) you will find that the distinction between the two terms is more nuanced than some texts would suggest.

> ## Thinking it through
>
> What might you explore in your inquiry: leadership or management or both?
>
> Do you agree with this distinction between leadership and management? To what extent do you see the two as linked?
>
> To what extent do you feel you and your colleagues have a sense that your institution is a joint enterprise?
>
> Do you feel, reading this, that your institution is over-managed or undermanaged?

Having established what we are inquiring into, we now go on to look at you: the reader and the inquirer.

Locating yourself in the picture

However much you will gain from sharing and discussing your inquiry with colleagues, inquiring is always in some sense a personal activity, especially if you are carrying out the inquiry as part of a course where you're assessed individually. However, even if this doesn't apply in your case at the moment, the inquiry still starts with you so it's important and useful to look inwards at least at the beginning.

Thinking about yourself as an inquirer

One of the first issues you will have to confront when starting to inquire is what we might call the difficulty of problematizing leadership and management where you work. After all, the institution where you are working is functioning at least in some sense, as a site of education. You may disagree in many ways with how you are led or managed, but how can you translate that feeling into an inquiry theme that will allow for the generation of evidence to support your views? At the same time, adopting a critical stance towards those in authority at your school might place yourself in contradiction to those who have made 'official' judgements. If OfSTED has rated your school as outstanding for leadership and management, on what basis might you defend your critique?

The answer here lies in defining and choosing your inquiry question carefully. Sometimes, the best inquiries involve taking a critical stance, in relation to practice or to the relationship between theory and practice. On the other hand, sometimes inquiries might look at how particular management strategies operate and not necessarily imply such a critical stance on your part. We discuss this sort of distinction below where we consider the distinction between monitoring and evaluation. The more what you are doing in your inquiry is evaluating, the more likely you are to be taking a critical stance towards decision making by yourself and by others. Inquiries that critique and challenge the status quo will perhaps be more stimulating inquiries for you to choose but they will require you to seek balance in what you write or present through generating and analysing evidence in support of your point of view and by using literature to bolster your case through comparing what you find with the thoughts and practice of others. The better you are able to harness rigorous research methodologies in your inquiry, the more you can legitimately take a critical stance towards practice at your school.

A helpful way of thinking here is to distinguish between doing research *on* or research *for* leadership and management. This comes down, in many ways, to a repeated theme of this book that it is helpful to distinguish between yourself as a researcher and yourself as an actor. Part of the success or otherwise of your inquiry will be about balancing the values you bring with you and perhaps your wish to change your institution with the need to let your data speak for itself; the need to apply some distance to your inquiry to look dispassionately at what is happening, what people are thinking before you consider any practical applications of your inquiry.

It's sometimes helpful to think carefully about yourself as an inquirer. After working with many teachers who have undertaken inquiries on their practice, Elaine Hall (2009) considers that the relationship that teacher inquirers have with theory develops as they gain experience of carrying out their own inquiries. Inquirers tend to become more critical and more autonomous in designing their methodology; in forming judgements about their own research and about what they read about the work of others. Thus you might well find that your appreciation of educational research in general will progress as you undertake more inquiries in your own school. You may also, she suggests, increasingly tend to trust your own judgement about how you plan and execute inquiries as well as becoming more sensitive to the complex reflexivities associated with exploring educational systems of which you yourself are a part.

> ## Thinking it through
>
> What do you think might be the consequences of carrying out a inquiry into a systems of which you are a part? How do you think this might make your inquiry easier or more difficult?
>
> How do you think the sort of judgements that researchers make differ from those made by, say OfSTED?
>
> Do you feel able to critique some of the research you read? If so, how?

Thinking about yourself as a leader

An obvious and powerful focus for your inquiry is your own leadership and management; whatever your position within your institution, there are rich possibilities here. So, if you hold a post of responsibility, you might explore the way you manage those you line manage. You could look at how you work in teams at your school; perhaps investigating peer coaching or observation and the culture underlying these activities. Another interesting dimension of teamwork that lends itself to investigation are your discussions in meetings and in more informal conversations. We'll look at language in the next section, but the content of what you do, and perhaps at least as interesting, what you do *not* talk about could be the starting point for an inquiry. Your attempts as a leader to influence a part of school culture would make another intriguing subject for a study. The leadership and management of non-teaching colleagues is an area where your inquiry could be sparked by the particularly rich literature that is available (see Peter Blatchford et al., 2009). Finally there's also a sense in which all who teach are leaders of those they teach: so you could design an inquiry around the way in which you inspire, organize and direct your students. These are just a few suggestions for investigation foci: you'll be able to think of many that are more appropriate to the particular challenges you face in your practice.

Looking 'close to home' at your own practice in this way has advantages and disadvantages. Many of the topics you might choose for an inquiry will require you to confront issues of ethics and sensitivity. It perhaps goes without saying that inquiring into the views of those you manage can present a technical challenge: how can you assure yourself of the validity (see Chapter 2 for a discussion of validity and reliability) of what you are told by people in such circumstances? Above all, however, personally focused inquiries like this have the potential to transform your practice in ways that looking at the work of others, however excellent that practice might be, will not have. Indeed, one might argue that there is a particular imperative in exploring your personal practice in leadership and management because what you do in this respect affects others directly.

So, putting yourself into your inquiry is important and to be encouraged but it's also good to talk these ideas through with colleagues as you go along. Collaborating with others in this way can enhance the impact of your work within the institution as well as helping you in designing and carrying out your inquiry. Equally, it is also important to broaden your thinking through reading.

Thinking it through

Consider the culture of observation in your setting. To what extent do you feel it is perceived to be supportive or threatening. By whom? How do you know this? How might you explore attitudes to observing and being observed in more depth?

Are there topics at your school or institution that are not talked about? Can you think of what you talk about most? Again, how do you know this and how might you explore this more rigorously?

The context for leadership in schools today

As you think about designing your inquiry into leadership and management, it will be helpful to think about the sorts of challenges and opportunities that will be and are now being experienced by those who lead in schools. As we write, there are still many unknowns about the various directions in which the continuous cycles of reform in education might lead but we have tried to identify some trends that appear likely to be a feature of the landscape within which schools will operate in the near future. Our aim in doing this is to help you think about some of the possible areas that you inquiry might explore: we have identified three broad themes here but you and your colleagues may well be able to identify others that are particularly relevant for your own institution.

First, schools are being encouraged and, in some senses required, as a result of funding changes to work collaboratively with other schools. At a formal level, schools may work together as federations or less formally they may cooperate, for example, in 'families' or 'pyramids' of schools. Schools that opt out of local authority control by becoming Academies for instance, may well find it advantageous or necessary to share resources between themselves and even those schools that stay within local authority control may be turning to neighbouring schools for services that are no longer offered centrally. Some of these associations between schools will involve collaboration by teaching staff, whether through joint planning or through the physical exchange of people. Such experiences provide rich material for inquiries and you might, for example, explore differences in culture and management structure and their effects on staff and student learning. You could choose to focus an inquiry on your own learning through immersion in a different institutional culture or you might wish to look at what you discover about and through coaching and mentoring in such situations. How can the same teachers influence colleagues in schools with differing cultures? How, for example, can middle leaders combine their roles as classroom teacher and departmental leader in one school with working in another school?

The second potential area for inquiry comes from the need for those in schools to work within a reduced level of resources: to 'do more with less'. This seems to be an inescapable necessity for schools for the immediate future and certainly a feature of the world with which leaders in your school; including you, will need to engage. As well as representing an obvious challenge to you as a teacher and leader, the squeeze on funding may also suggest avenues of inquiry. Analysing the effect in terms of value for money of programmes, interventions or pupil groupings, for example, could be a productive basis for an inquiry with clear practical links to school leadership. This is an area which would lend itself particularly well to a quantitative study (see Chapter 2 for more on this sort of inquiry) in which you could attempt to dissect the reasons underlying why some pupils make more progress than others or the complex relationship between costs and benefits in education.

A third area which schools are being increasingly asked to develop and which is ideally suited to teacher inquiry is the critical analysis and development of in-school monitoring and evaluation. By *monitoring*, we mean the oversight of how a system operates; whereas *evaluation* implies a more critical appraisal of current systems perhaps with a view to replacing those systems. In your inquiry, by definition, you will almost certainly be evaluating whereas in the school, on a day-to-day basis, there will probably be much more monitoring taking place. Schools are involved in monitoring in a number of senses: the monitoring of pupils and staff is a routine part of school life, evaluation maybe less so. There is ample potential for you to explore or adapt both of these processes for your inquiry. For example, you could evaluate how outcomes are monitored in your school and the methodologies used for measuring attainment and progress. Educational research has much to offer (for a review, see Mike Wallace and Louise Poulson, 2003) in informing the ways in which you define, generate new evidence, reassess existing school data or rigorously analyse outcomes. Inquiries in this area have obvious practical application to yourself and to your school; not least in developing the capacity for rigorous and honest self-evaluation.

So the ever-changing environment in education offers some promising themes for you to address through your inquiries and we hope that this book as a whole will help you form these ideas into investigations. Researching in this area, as we will see later this chapter, is not without its difficulties but inquiries into leadership and management in your own school have great potential to change and reframe the way in which you think about your practice.

However important it is to look to your own practice when developing your inquiry, one of the characteristics of leadership and management as a field is that educators have tended to reach outside teaching for ideas on leadership and the cross fertilization of ideas from beyond education has been an important influence at many levels within the profession. In the next section we'll look at a case study which drew on thinking from a perhaps unexpected source.

Thinking it through

What are the opportunities and challenges posed when schools work collaboratively in your experience?

Think about the way in which the discussions about resources have been framed in your institution. Who had led and who has contributed to these discussions? How would you characterize this process and what might that suggest about your school?

How might and how do leaders influence the teaching and learning taking place in your school? How much influence do you yourself have in this respect?

Case study: Leading whole-school change

Stefan wanted to carry out an inquiry into leadership at his school. He was particularly interested in exploring the impact of an innovative way of thinking that had been recently adopted by the senior leadership team at the school. A year previously, the Headteacher had learnt about the 'Blue Ocean Strategy' (you can read about this in Chan-Kim and Mauborgne, 2003): a way of identifying obstacles to change, categorizing them as relating to understanding, resources, motivation or politics. The Head explained the strategy to colleagues at a staff meeting, pointing out this approach is predicated on limited resources and is therefore most suitable in the current financial climate.

The school focused its use of the strategy on literacy across the curriculum and in its pastoral structures. Every year the school was receiving students new into Year 7 with low literacy levels. Written-based subjects such as History and English had been suffering from falling or stagnating results for two to three years. In response, the school wanted to create a culture based on developing literate students.

The school leadership addressed the four parts of the Blue Ocean Strategy as follows. They had attended to the cognitive hurdles by carefully explaining the change process to subject leaders and governors so school leaders were sure that everybody understood the nature of and reasons for the change. The 'resource hurdles' were circumvented by reallocating funding from other projects. Motivation for the literacy initiative among staff and students was bolstered by inviting famous authors to speak and by senior leaders modelling a literacy culture through reading to tutor groups. Finally, potential political hurdles were addressed by, for example, reassuring the maths teachers that resources would be directed their way in the following year.

In his inquiry, Stefan had to choose whether to evaluate the Blue Ocean Strategy itself; which would essentially be a leadership question, or the way in which the strategy was applied, which would have made his more of a management inquiry. He chose the former. Reading about leadership (using Mike Wallace and Louise Poulson's 2003 book in particular), Stefan came to see that the point about models such as the Blue Ocean Strategy is not so much whether they are in any sense 'true' as a description of a change process, the critical question is more about whether they are helpful for leaders in thinking about those processes. This understanding helped him to draw up a list of questions about how the strategy was chosen, whether any alternatives were considered and so on. Stefan turned these questions into an interview script and then approached the Headteacher.

Stefan was aware of the difficulty of interviewing his own Headteacher about a strategy that had been adopted by the school and which was generally regarded as having been successful. He therefore took great pains to explain to the Headteacher why he had chosen this particular inquiry focus. Stefan made it clear that he was interested in the intellectual processes behind the way in which the Head had led this initiative. The interview was very productive and Stefan was able to draw conclusions which could be summarized as follows: that the power of such a strategy lies, not so much in the fact that it makes decisions any easier or any different than they would be without such a guide. Stefan concluded that the Blue Ocean Strategy, more than being an analytical framework had really been a 'story' that had explained and reassured about change. He was able to support this interpretation using extracts from the interview with the Head.

Having thought carefully about his choice of methodology, Stefan was clear that his choice of a case study approach was the right one here (see Chapter 2 for more on such decisions); although he had only interviewed one person, he felt that was entirely appropriate given what he was investigating. Finally, Stefan was aware of the potential sensitivity of this piece of research so he did not disseminate it among colleagues and took great care to anonymize his account of this inquiry when he submitted it to his university tutor.

Thinking it through

Choose a process of change that has happened to your school recently. Can you identify the various 'hurdles' to change that have been overcome or still exist?

What do you think that models like this achieve? When they are effective, to what do you attribute their success?

What do you think are the advantages and dangers of applying models from non-educational settings like this?

Next we offer a selection of some theoretical insights drawn from recent research literature that may help you to think differently about your inquiries. The chapter concludes with a second case study.

Some perspectives on leadership and management

Power and language

In some ways you may perhaps be only too aware of the potential influence of power on your inquiry. The opinions and practices of those in authority are in some senses invested with a particular weight which, as we have seen above, can present challenges to those inquiring into leadership and management. Identifying and describing where and how power is being used, however, can transform your understanding of your organization and provide robust support for the critiques of leadership and management that you construct. One of the less obvious ways in which that power may be enacted is through the language that people use. As Michel Foucault and others have observed, knowledge is power, and language the means by which that power is transmitted. One approach to inquiring into leadership and management is to take careful notice of the words that people use. Thinkers about this sometimes use the term *discourses:* which you can think of as the shared stories that people are 'allowed' to tell about organizations, about each other or about themselves. At the most obvious level, these discourses can be what appear in a prospectus or a school self-evaluation: at a more subtle level, these can be reflected in how you talk with colleagues about inclusion, for example.

Discourses in effect embody the 'taken for granteds' in an institution, delimiting what can be said, and tending to make it difficult or unacceptable to act or even think outside these limits. It perhaps could to be said at this stage that such Orwellian descriptions of discourse may seem exaggerated and perhaps not 'ring true' as descriptions of conversations you might be having with colleagues who might well be personal friends. It's fair to say that many of the discourses you might identify in your setting can be quite mundane and may not tell you much about the effects of power within you setting. Do not, however, dismiss discourse as an analytical tool: you may identify ways of speaking and thinking that perhaps unexpectedly reflect something about the way your school is led or the way you lead yourself that would not be obvious or apparent unless you allow yourself to think in this way. This is why discourse analysis can be a powerful tool for understanding your own organization. You can find a more detailed discussion of discourse analysis in the context of inclusion in Linda Dunn's 2009 paper. For an example of this technique in leadership and management, there is an interesting paper by Julia Ibbotson (2007) which looks at the differences in the language used by male and female school middle leaders.

The importance of feelings

Again, this may seem to be self evident but we felt it worth including here a reminder that there is a substantial body of research suggesting that how people feel (the *affective*) in an organization matters just as much as what they think (the *cognitive*). Exploring colleague's feelings is therefore a potentially productive if not entirely straightforward way to gather evidence for your inquiry. Like discourse analysis above, the exploration of the affective in your colleagues is capable of allowing you to see systems and relationships in a different light. The key to inquiring in this way, as Megan Crawford and Chris James (2006) point out is to look not so much at the feelings or affects themselves but rather at the how feelings influence what people do. In other words to explore explanations of why people do what they do, not in cognitive terms but in terms of 'gut feelings', of 'instincts' or 'what felt right'.

Remembering what matters

Finally, we come to a way in which your inquiries can make a difference both within your institution and beyond. There is little doubt that research into leadership and management in schools does matter because evidence (Phillip Hallinger and Richard Heck, 2003) shows that leadership and management make a real difference to school performance. Well-led schools consistently outperform poorly led schools (McKinsey, 2007). The problem with the evidence base in this area is, as Stephen Gorard (2005) points out, that it tells us most about the influence of management *on itself* and least about the influence of management on pupil performance, on pupil progress, on how pupils feel about their time at school. What professional researchers have done therefore is to largely ignore what really matters in education. As a result, we know that well-led schools are better but since we don't really know what 'well led' means in terms of what pupils experience, this knowledge by itself isn't very helpful. This is perhaps why when you come to look at literature on school leadership and management, you will read a lot of 'think pieces' and opinion articles with very little evidence to support what is written.

So there is the challenge to you in your inquiries: to look inside the leadership and management of your school or institution, perhaps inside your own leadership and management, but to do so remembering that neither are an end in themselves.

Thinking it through

Think about your inquiry and the way you present it. How might you address two different audiences, the internal and the external, for example, colleagues and university tutors?

We have talked very little about inquiry methods in this chapter. Take a look at Chapters 2 and 3: what methods do you think would lend themselves to this topic?

Case study: Leading on maths

Gillian is an experienced Year 5 teacher in a primary school in the north of England. Two years ago, she took on responsibility for coordinating maths in the school. When, the following year she completed her masters degree with a final module on leadership and management, Gillian constructed an inquiry around the way she carried out this role.

First of all, Gillian needed to look at a focus for this inquiry. Being quite new to the role of a coordinator, Gillian felt that she would gain most from an inquiry that helped her in supporting the professional development of her colleagues in this area. This was a key area of the role and one for which she still felt somewhat unprepared.

Helped by her university tutor, Gillian found the 2010 report by the National Centre for Excellence in the Teaching of Mathematics (NCETM, 2010) particularly helpful. She read and summarized the findings of the report and highlighted some of the points arising. She was particularly interested to read the authors' suggestion that a cycle of collaborative activity between colleagues based around lesson planning, predicting pupil responses to maths activities, teaching and reflection had been shown to be an effective means of CPD. Gillian took up this idea and decided 1) to suggest to colleagues that they adopt this approach to developing their maths teaching; and 2) to plan her inquiry around trying to confirm or challenge the findings of the NCETM report.

During a staff meeting, Gillian circulated a section of the NCETM report, explained what she had read and asked colleagues to consider adopting this approach. She was conscious of the need to give her fellow teachers at the school a choice in that way but she also understood that her choice of inquiry rested on their agreement! Fortunately, they all agreed to try this approach and Gillian was able with little difficulty to incorporate this structure into the fortnightly planning meetings that were already held to coordinate planning in maths and other subjects.

To generate data for the inquiry, Gillian decided on a mixture of questionnaires and examining pupil work. She was also aware that pupil attainment data might be helpful but her tutor warned her not to expect to be able simply to link pupil progress to her initiative when there could be so many other factors influencing pupil learning. Gillian then had to think carefully about the sorts of questions to ask her colleagues. This was difficult when so much of what was happening was being discussed in meetings anyway. She found it helpful to keep coming back to the 'what would be happening if this approach were working?' question. So Gillian looked to measure colleagues' confidence in teaching Maths, their willingness to take risks and try new things, at what they were noticing about pupils now they were consciously being asked by Gillian to make more detailed evaluations of pupil learning.

Gillian used a Likert scale (see Chapters 2 and 3) questionnaire together with some extended answer questions to measure attitudes (she made sure colleagues understood clearly that they were not being judged in any way on what they wrote). Her colleagues completed this at the start of a term and then again at the end. Gillian also encouraged them to jot down anything that happened in maths lessons that might be relevant to the study. Looking at the questionnaire responses, pupils' work and test results at the end of the term, Gillian was delighted to find that both the teachers and pupils seemed (and felt themselves) to have made progress. When she wrote up the inquiry, Gillian was also able to reflect on her own leadership and management of the project: this was made much easier as she had kept an inquiry diary throughout the term.

Drawing it together

- Appreciating the distinction between leadership and management can be helpful in focusing your inquiry. You might also find it helpful to think about the processes of monitoring and evaluation when you draw up a question and an appropriate methodology

- It's also helpful to think about yourself as an inquirer. How do you fit into your organization? How do you lead and manage? What matters to you individually?
- Think about the challenges facing your school and how these might be developed into an inquiry focus: inquiring into what matters for your institution.
- Remember a weakness of much of what is written about leadership and management is a lack of evidence. Look at the case studies here in conjunction with Chapters 2 and 3 and when you write, try to support your work with evidence.
- Think about issues of power, language and feelings. They are all ways to get behind what people say 'officially' about what they do. They might suggest ways in which you can start to access what people really think.

References

Bennett, N. et al. (2003) *Distributed Leadership: A Review of Literature.* Open University/National College for School Leadership. Available at: http://oro.open.ac.uk/8534/1/bennett-distributed-leadership-full.pdf (Accessed 27-Aug-11).

Blatchford, P. et al. (2009) *The Deployment and Impact of Support Staff.* DCFS Research Brief DCSF-RB148. Available at www.schoolsupportstaff.net/publications/DISS_reports/DISS_Res_Sum.pdf (Accessed 23-Jul-11).

Bush, T. and Middlewood, D. (2005) *Leading and Managing People in Education.* London: Sage.

Chan-Kim, W. and Mauborgne, R. (2003) Tipping Point Leadership. *Harvard Business Review April 2003.*

Crawford, M. and James, C. (2006) *An Affective Paradigm for Educational Leadership and Management Practice and Research.* Paper presented at BERA 2007. Available at www.leeds.ac.uk/educol/documents/160642.htm (Accessed 25-Jul-11).

Dunn, L. (2009) Discourses of inclusion: a critique. *Power and Education,* Vol. 1 No. 1, pp. 42–56.

Gorard, S. (2005) Current contexts for research in educational leadership and management. *Educational Management Administration & Leadership,* Vol. 33, No. 2, pp. 155–64.

Hall, E. (2009) Engaging in and engaging with research: teacher inquiry and development. *Teachers and Teaching: Theory and Practice,* Vol. 15, No. 6, pp. 669–81.

Hallinger, P. and Heck, R. (2003) Understanding the contribution of leadership to school improvement. In Wallace, M. and Poulson, L. *Learning to Read Critically in Educational Leadership and Management.* London: Sage.

Higgins, S., Kokotsaki, D. and Coe, R. (2011) *Toolkit of Strategies to Improve Learning,* Sutton Trust. Available at http://www.suttontrust.com/public/documents/toolkit-summary-final-r-2-.pdf (Accessed 31-Aug-11).

Ibbotson, J. (2007) *Management-Speak: Implications of Research into the Connections between Management Communication, School Ethos and Professional Development Observed in Communities of Educational Practice in the Secondary School Sector.* Paper presented at BERA 2007. Available at www.leeds.ac.uk/educol/documents/165678.htm (Accessed 25-Jul-11).

Mckinsey (2007) *How the World's Best Performing School Systems Come Out on Top.* Available at www.mckinsey.com/App_Media/Reports/SSO/Worlds_School_Systems_Final.pdf (Accessed 28-Aug-11).

National Centre for Excellence in the Teaching of Mathematic. (2010) *Assessing the Impact of the National Centre for Excellence in the Teaching of Mathematics (NCETM) on Teachers and Learners. Executive Summary of the Final Report.* Centre for Education and Inclusion Research Sheffield Hallam University. Available at: https://www.ncetm.org.uk/files/6448759/Executive+Summary+04+06+10.pdf (Accessed 6/10/2011).

Wallace, M. and Poulson, L. (2003) *Learning to Read Critically in Educational Leadership and Management.* London: Sage.

Part 3
Sharing your Findings

Presenting Teacher Inquiry

Nick Mitchell and Joanne Pearson

Chapter Outline

Introduction

This chapter is about presenting your inquiry. We will discuss why it's important and advantageous to share your work with others, what you should bear in mind about presenting your work and how you can make doing this easier and more meaningful. While we shall mostly be concerned with writing as a means of presentation, we will also refer to the many other ways in which you can involve others in discussing your work. So while this chapter is aimed at helping you put together an individual presentation of your inquiry, we always encourage you to approach presenting your work as an opportunity to discuss the things that matter to you in your practice with your colleagues.

There are many other texts that describe the practicalities of 'writing up' teacher inquiry in more detail than we are able to accommodate here. Among others we would recommend: *The Good Writing Guide for Education Students* (2007) by Dominic Wyse, *a Guide to Practitioner Research in Education* (2011) by Ian Menter et al. and *Teachers Investigate Their Work* (2008) by Herbert Altricher et al. In spite of all this excellent advice, however, we are aware that for many teachers, especially those following professional development courses, 'writing up' their research is often seen as a demanding and challenging imposition. So while we will cover some of the same ground as these texts we are also hoping here as in the rest of this book to communicate something of the satisfaction and sense of personal development that can flow from sharing the ideas in your teacher inquiries.

A theme running thoughout this book has been the importance of inquiring into what matters personally to you and to your practice. The more fundamentally your work is grounded in what you do as a practitioner, the more you should be able to engage in that inquiry and to defend and justify what you present at the end. At the same time, teacher inquiry works best when it is a *collaborative* activity helping you to develop understanding that you can share and discuss with others. We will next look briefly at why sharing your work is important and then move on to suggest the practical steps you can take towards presenting your inquiry effectively.

Thinking it through

What experiences have you had of 'presenting' to colleagues rather than teaching? How do you think the two activities differ?

What are your experiences of reading or seeing research presented to you?

Why presenting your work matters

To an extent, you may have little choice about presenting your work. If you are carrying out your inquiry as part of a professional development course you will be expected to show your work to your tutors, usually in the form of a written assignment. There are strong arguments, however, why you as a teacher should in any event share the outcomes of your classroom inquiries more widely.

Two strong arguments in favour of teacher inquiry are, first, that teachers are still underrepresented in academic and professional literature and as a result, many teachers find it hard to see the connection between literature on education and everyday teacher practice. Second, the sharing of inquiries that teachers undertake can also be seen as one way of preserving and disseminating many classroom practices that might otherwise not be shared and practical knowledge lost (Menter et al., 2011).

On a personal level, inquiring into the classroom has, as we hope other chapters in this book will illustrate, the potential to transform your practice and that of others. As you go through the process of turning your thoughts into text, you will be developing your understanding of the relationship between educational theory and practice. You will be generating your own theory (because educational theory is no more than descriptions of practice) as well as engaging with the theory of others. Carrying out an inquiry in the classroom will help you to reflect on your own practice, but will also help you when you read and hear others talking about their practice. Remember that many of the ideas you will find in academic literature are difficult not so much because they are inherently complex, but because they are not usually discussed by practising teachers.

Thinking it through

Choose a recent educational initiative that you have implemented. Did it work in your classroom? Why do you say this? How might you go about showing this?

Can you think of an example of something from your own practice that you feel might be shared more widely? What in particular makes you think of this example and how might you prove this to others?

In the next section, we look at academic writing and how it relates to the way in which you might present your own work.

How to present your work

What we have discussed above will hopefully have convinced you that presenting your work to others is important. The next section will help you think about how to present your inquiry. Most of what follows is about writing because that will be the most likely way in which you will choose or be required to present your work, but we will go on to examine additional means of presentation.

You will probably have begun to read academic texts well before you start to write about your inquiry and you would be unusual if you were not struck by the difference between what you read in such articles and the style in which you yourself feel you are able to write. There are two things to say here. First, you should realize that this feeling is actually a sign that you are engaged in learning to do something that is, by its nature, difficult and which requires you to learn and develop a set of high-level skills. Second, you should understand that it is entirely appropriate that there should be a distinction between your style and that of published academic articles. While you should look to emulate some aspects of the work that you read, you should also recognize that the way you write about teacher inquiry should quite rightly be different and personal to you.

If you think about the everyday informal conversations that you have with colleagues and pupils during the course of a day, the language as you use it here is not always appropriate for presenting a classroom inquiry but crucially, it will often have an energy and an immediate connection with practice and practical problems that can easily be lost when this 'practitioner' speak is turned into academic language. The challenge is to take this fluid, unreflective, emotion-laden, subjective knowledge that is developed through practitioner conversations and to translate that often tacit understanding into balanced and critical accounts. There is therefore a translation process between the fleeting thoughts and impressions you have as you teach or reflect or talk about your practice and the more considered language you will use in writing about your inquiry. It is this translation process you should always have in your mind when you write and present your inquiry: trying to capture the immediacy of practice in reflective writing, balancing and combining the best of both. Incidentally, this is another reason why you should not necessarily take all academic writing as a model because even experienced, highly respected writers do not always manage to achieve this difficult transformation.

Beyond the aim of representing classroom practice in what you write, there is another reason why your writing and presentation should not necessarily resemble published academic writing. As Marilyn Cochran-Smith and Susan Lytle (2009) write, the knowledge you gain from classroom inquiries may be used as a means of challenging practices and structures within and beyond your own school. Writing and presenting such inquiries requires something outside the normal confines of academic literature: it requires you to find your personal voice to express the sometimes sensitive outcomes of research into your practice, maybe addressing difficult issues of democracy or social justice. Although academic writers certainly do tackle these sorts of questions, in your inquiry you will be focusing on *your* setting in the here and now. The immediacy of this connection between your practice and your inquiry will give you a powerful and unique standpoint in discussing practices which are specific to your school or which are just starting to evolve. In short, you have the potential to be more controversial and more relevant than academic authors.

Thinking it through

In what ways does the task of presenting an inquiry resemble or differ from journalism or fiction writing or broadcasting?

Look at a magazine or the television news. How do they get their message across and what might you learn that you could apply to writing about your inquiry?

Writing

If you are carrying out your inquiry as part of a course, then you should have the format of how you present your work specified for you. It is important to realize, however, that even if you are doing your classroom inquiry as part of a masters course, you will have considerable freedom in the way in which you approach writing about your work. It is important for you to establish a good working relationship with your tutor(s) and to reach a common understanding about how your work should be presented, but it is also necessary for you to find a way to write that you feel actually expresses what you want to say: you should never feel that the structure you are following is restrictive.

Let's start at the beginning, however. Here is a guide to writing about your inquiry. First, we help you start out on writing up your inquiry, then we look at how to plan out your account. We then focus on the qualities that your writing should aim to show and we finish with hints on writing style.

Starting to write

The experience of many teachers as they contemplate starting to write about their inquiry is, we suspect, not always pleasant; dominated by the horror of that first blank page, the looming bulk of the enormous word count and by the thought that you are being asked to produce something original that will be seen, read or in some way judged by others. Faced with this, it is invaluable to have a belief in the worth of what you are wanting to say, and a set of tactics to help you get started and sustain you through the first few weeks of the project. Hopefully the first will flow from your choice of an inquiry that matters to you personally, as we have discussed above. As for the second, here are some suggestions for ways to kick-start your writing. Although planning out your work is vital, you are likely to find that just getting started and writing a few sentences that get you thinking about some of the issues around your inquiry is an easier way to start than drawing up a plan right away.

- As soon as you possibly can, write small 'scraps'. These can be paragraphs, sentences or even shorter collections of words. These may come out of keeping a journal as you go through your inquiry (you can read more about doing this in Chapter 2 or they may just be writing down yourself thinking aloud. The scraps may come from an initial response to looking at a questionnaire or listening to an interview, they may be your first reactions to reading something. However they come, writing scraps means you have started the writing and you might well go on to use what you write in this way in the final product, but even if you don't, it will probably have helped you when you do come to write.
- From the beginning, talk about your inquiry with colleagues, partners or anybody who will listen. Discussing what you are doing is a great way to organize your thinking and clarify your meaning. If you can explain your work to somebody else informally then you are much more likely to be able to do so formally in writing or in a presentation.
- Engage with your writing. If this means writing out a 'rant' about an issue then do so; it will get your mind working on what to say. Your final presentation of the inquiry will need to be balanced and measured but the same doesn't necessarily apply to your early drafts. Your writing can be refined later on and we suggest below some ways to do this but it is far more important, particularly if you are new to writing and presenting classroom inquiry, to get your ideas out on paper rather than to always write in a 'correct' way.

Having started and hopefully with some words down on paper, the next step is to begin to organize those thoughts and writings.

Planning

The way you plan writing about your inquiry will depend in part on how experienced you are and it might also vary depending upon the guidance, if any, that you have been given. You may perhaps have been supplied with an outline suggesting how to divide up your work or you may be entirely free to design your account. The process of planning, however, is essentially always the same: start with large headings and then subdivide these into smaller headings.

If you can carry on doing this until you reach the level of paragraphs, your text is more likely to read like a connected meaningful piece of writing. Of course the process will probably be much messier than we have made it sound here: there will be dead ends, deletions, additions and rewriting along the way but if you can come up with a skeleton for your work, you can begin to insert some of the 'scraps' you have written (see above) and your work will then begin to take on a shape and, if you have one, the word count you have been set will not seem quite so distant.

Don't be worried about changing your plan. You may have to do this in response to comments by a tutor or by a colleague or you may feel yourself that some parts of your account just aren't working. It is always difficult and slightly painful to have to lose sections you have written or change around what you thought was finished, but rethinking and replanning in this way nearly always produces a better piece of work in the end.

Thinking it through

Look at a piece of academic writing or a practitioner account of an inquiry and pick out the structure the writer has used. Look in particular at the different levels of heading used. Do you think there are too many or too few?

Six things to aim for

It sounds so obvious, but it needs saying, that the purpose of writing and presenting your work is to express what you mean to say. Particularly when you are new to writing of this sort, you may be particularly concerned with using the right language and with the presentation of your work: the line spacing, the way you reference etc. If you are producing a piece of coursework, these should be specified for you and you should try to make sure that you follow the advice you are given. We would also recommend Dominic Wyse (2007) for clear advice on referencing and grammar. What we want to do in this section, however, is to look more generally at how you can present your ideas most clearly and powerfully. Following the six pieces of advice here will not only assist you to do this but will also help you as you go along to understand the ideas themselves more clearly.

Support your work with evidence from your practice

Your writing will be more authoritative and persuasive if you support your claims with evidence. As you write, it's a good discipline to ask yourself as you go along how you might be able to justify each point you make. In Chapters 2 and 3 you can see some of the sorts of evidence that you might reference and include in order to do this. Consider the following extract from a teacher's account of an inquiry.

> *Lavender High has a highly supportive staff, which sees each child as unique and is eager to support each individual in the classroom setting.*

This is an example of the sort of writing containing generalized statements that are difficult or impossible to support with evidence. Compare that statement with the one that follows which is much more specific: unlike the first, this second statement can readily be supported with evidence.

> *A breakdown of our SEN register shows that there is a higher proportion of children of Asian heritage plus in Foundation and Key Stage 1 than of Afro-Caribbean heritage (see table 1).*

Support your work with reference to literature

In Chapter 1, you can see more about how to reference literature in support of your work and any search of the internet will readily turn up workable guides to Harvard referencing, the preferred system in educational publications. Referencing is a standard part of writing and presenting but it's important for you to realize just why this is considered good practice. When you draw on the work of other authors, you increase the credibility of what you write by showing that your thoughts are, at least in some way, shared by others whose work has been published. Using literature in this way is also, of course, a way of extending your own thinking but also of expanding the vocabulary that you use. You may do this by using direct quotes (which must of course be attributed to their author to avoid *plagiarism*) or by drawing on the terms that you come across in literature in sections you write yourself. Either way, the result is to enrich your text and to vary the register used.

> *SENCos are also expected to undertake extrinsic activities for which they feel unprepared and which were outside the aspects of the role that Prather-Jones (2010) found to be associated with motivation and job satisfaction.*

Write critically

Something to develop in your writing as you gain experience is *criticality*. This is important not only for work for masters courses, where writing critically is usually a learning outcome, but the discipline of thinking critically is a skill that will help you in your professional development more generally. There are many competing descriptions of what 'criticality' in writing actually means (e.g., Andrew Stables, 2003; Wilf Carr and Andrew Kemmis 2005) and there are many ways in which you can be critical; for example:

- You might be critical of practices at your institution.

  The interviews I conducted with pupils as part of my inquiry suggest that the setting policy at the school may have some unexpected and undesired consequences for pupil motivation and engagement.

- You might be critical of nationally accepted practices.

  From carrying out this inquiry, I have begun to question whether plenary sessions are always a necessary part of a 'good' lesson.

- You might be critical of the data that you have generated (see Chapters 2 and 3) as part of your inquiry.

  Eighteen pupils completed questionnaires but analysing their responses, I am doubtful about the extent to which these have been a reliable way of gathering data: many seem to have been filled in hurriedly and with little apparent thought.

- You might be critical of what has been written in academic literature as a result of what you have found out in your inquiry.

  The findings of this inquiry into the effects of pupil grouping raise questions about the large-scale study by Sooty and Sweep (2010). Their work did not consider relationships between teacher and pupils to be an important factor: this inquiry suggests otherwise.

- Or you might be critical of what academics have written on its own merits.

The argument that Morecambe (1997) puts forward about the value of teaching assistants in classrooms is clearly contradicted by what Wise (2000) writes. Morecambe's work also appears to rest largely on his own classroom observation: the words of teaching assistants themselves do not appear anywhere in his article.

Be balanced

Criticality, then, is a thing to be encouraged when you write and present your inquiry. Like most good things in life, however, it does need to be tempered and controlled. The most persuasive and impressive accounts of an inquiry will usually seem balanced and reasonable commentaries on your practice, not polemics against your school or the powers that be. Thankfully, there are three practical steps you can take to balance your writing and you should have these in the back of your mind, particularly when you come towards a final version of your text or presentation.

First, acknowledge what you don't know. Sprinkle your work with softeners like 'perhaps', 'suggests', 'indicates', 'potentially', 'my small study implies', and avoid 'always', 'never', 'proves', 'shows', 'must', 'causes' and 'conclusive'. There is always room for doubt about your inquiry findings (even if you don't really believe there is), so leave the door open with these sorts of words. Secondly, try if possible to suggest other interpretations of your data or your conclusions. You can and wherever possible should still show personal conviction about your preferred reading of the evidence but actually that will usually come over more strongly if you can present an alternative and show the superiority of your interpretation; for example,

As we have seen, my data suggest that these sorts of activities can contribute to pupil engagement in maths lessons although it is conceivable that at least some of the effects that I have described might be simply due to the extra attention I have paid to this particular group over the last school term.

The third practical suggestion to add balance to your work is to include a qualification paragraph (and/or presentation slide) somewhere near the end pointing out that what you have presented is a small scale study that might or might not be representative of practice in other classrooms.

Be selective

It's likely that when you come to write about and present your work, you will be concerned that you are going to leave things out: that you need to make sure that everything that you've found or thought or read is included in your account. This is perfectly understandable but this approach can result in writing and presentations that are both rushed and cluttered. Instead you should aim for quality and coherence over quantity and completeness. If you have, say, six findings from your inquiry, see if you can choose the most important three or the three which connect best with what you have read about the subject. Two or three significant findings, properly explained and supported with literature and evidence, are generally the most that you can fit into a 5,000-word piece of writing. This may surprise you at first, but it's true!

Anonymize

In the introduction to this book, you will find a discussion of some of the ethical issues that you will need to think about as part of your inquiry. As we have suggested, part of the rationale for writing is to share your work with colleagues and perhaps with a wider audience but in sharing your work, you need to make sure that confidential details are not passed on either directly (through actually including them) or indirectly (by, for instance, making the identity of a pupil obvious). One of the most obvious ways to anonymize is to use pseudonyms (which are harder to make up than you might think) for the people and institutions involved in your inquiry. Another check you should always carry out is to make sure that details on letterheads, and so on, are blanked out in any documents that you include in appendices.

Thinking it through

Look through a piece of your writing and ask, 'what am I absolutely sure about here?' Then think about the 'softeners' you might insert to show you are leaving room for doubt.

Practise your criticality: find a piece of writing or a broadcast about education that really irks you! Then try to think why this should be so and to find the flaws in what is said.

⇨

Thinking it through—Cont'd

Work backwards. Look at a piece of evidence from your practice: a lesson plan or some pupil work perhaps. Ask yourself what you might be able to show from this: pupil engagement, relationships and so on. This should help when you think about trying to support what you write with evidence.

Writing in a good style

It's entirely possible for you to do all the things we recommended in the last section and still present your work in a way that is hard to follow and therefore unconvincing. You also need to think about your style or, in other words, how to make your work flowing and interesting for your audience. So while attending to everything we have suggested up to now should have made yours a sound piece of work, the following suggestions will help you refine that into something that reads and sounds better not only to you, but crucially, to your audience.

Signpost the reader

Because *you* know what you mean, there is a tendency to expect the reader to know what you are trying to say. Simply starting sections with a brief summary of what you are intending to say, and sometimes (although perhaps not as often) ending sections with a summary of what has been said, is helpful to readers. What's more, it may help you to organize your writing and give you a head start when it comes to writing conclusions at the end of your work.

Write actively not passively

Reading academic literature, you will often come across passive sentences such as: *questionnaires were completed by pupils* or *there is a negative attitude among students to extended writing in ICT*. These are, of course, quite acceptable forms of expression and they do communicate meaning clearly but you may find that you will write more fluently and easily if you change these sentences around to make them active. By this I mean that you make a person or people the subject of the sentence. Hence these two examples become *pupils completed questionnaires* and *students show a negative attitude to extended writing in ICT*.

Don't be afraid to use 'I'

An effective way to make your writing more active is to use the first person. As we have seen, one of the objectives of writing and presenting your work is to engage personally with the issues into which you are inquiring and the most direct way to do this is to write from a personal standpoint using the first person.

Try to find simpler ways to say what you wish to say

If you are struggling with your writing, it may be that you are overcomplicating what you are trying to say. Take a small section – a paragraph perhaps – and write out what you mean to say in the simplest, ugliest, most everyday words you can. When you have done this, you will probably have clarified what you want to convey and you can then just work on saying it in a prettier way! Another technique is to dictate into a recorder or phone (perhaps using voice recognition software to transcribe what you say). Most of us speak in a simpler and clearer way than we write, so thinking aloud like this is another way to unscramble your thinking.

Break your writing up using subheadings and paragraphs

This may seem an obvious point or a merely cosmetic suggestion, but dividing your work up with subheadings and writing in smaller paragraphs can be helpful in structuring your thoughts as well as making your work easier to read and to turn into a presentation. Dominic Wyse (2007) suggests a subheading every 500 words and I would say aim for paragraphs about the size of this one you're now reading. You might even find it helpful to give each paragraph its own sub-subheading: by doing this and planning what you are saying in fine detail, you'll help avoid repetitions and big leaps from one topic to another. Once you have written the paragraph, you can always remove the headings if you wish.

Use people's words

Writing for academic purposes should always be about presenting or selling a story, and good storytellers make their work vivid by using the real words of others in the form of word for word quotations. Verbatim quotes capture the flavour of what people say and think much more effectively than any paraphrasing of their words, it varies the register of what you write and helps you concentrate on the small details that can be just as important as the big picture. You will have analysed your interview data before you come to write about your findings and presenting this analysis will be an important part of what you write but where possible you should include actual quotes. Look at these examples of pupils' words and you will appreciate how powerfully they convey the child's view.

> I don't like writing when it's a long story.
>
> I would be happier in school if there were less grumpy teachers.
>
> When I woke up it felt like I had fireworks in my tummy because I was so excited.

Thinking it through

Try talking through and recording your thoughts about a section of your plan or even about the whole thing.

Look at the text of this book. Are we practising what we preach on style?

Read out part of your work to a colleague or friend. Does this suggest anything about how clearly you are writing?

If possible look at written accounts of inquiries by other teachers, perhaps those who are writing the same assignment as you. Choose one or two of these style points to focus on and try to improve on what you see.

Sharing your work with others

In this chapter so far, we have talked about writing as a means of presenting your work but I hope we have also stressed that the end product of your inquiry should not be written work, in fact it should not even be a presentation of that work through a talk or seminar. The end point of your inquiry, if there is one, should be the discussion that continues with your colleagues after your inquiry is completed written up and shared. In one sense, your inquiry 'succeeds' to the extent that this has happened and you should have this in mind in the way you approach presenting and discussing your work. Of course, the process of sharing your inquiry should start from when you begin to plan and carry on throughout the inquiry. We have encouraged you throughout this book to discuss what you are doing with colleagues and presenting the end product should be simply an extension of this.

There are many ways in which you might consider sharing your work. We will finish by briefly looking at four possible ways of doing this.

Posters

You might display your work in a poster form to publicize your research in your school or perhaps as a presentation at a conference. Sharing your work in school like this is a practical way to make others aware of your inquiries, possibly stimulating discussions and involving pupils in what you are doing. Apart from the interest in the investigation, you should not underestimate the effect of the message that teachers like you are asking questions about their practice in this way. Posters may also be used for presentation at conferences: for advice on poster design see Ian Menter et al. (2011).

Presentations

The most straightforward way of turning your written work into something you can share is through turning it into a presentation. As we have hinted in this chapter so far, a well-structured piece of writing easily lends itself to being divided up into a series of PowerPoint slides. Going back, however, to the reason for the presentation, you should try always to raise questions for discussion as much as present what you yourself have found in your inquiry. Remember also that the methods you have used to inquire may be of particular interest to others who may be tackling their own inquiries. It may not be your first instinct when presenting, but one of the most important reasons for giving a presentation is to make use of it as a way of testing and validating your work. An inquiry that provokes thought in your colleagues will always be a valuable and worthwhile inquiry whatever its findings.

Electronic sharing

There is a wide and growing number of ways in which you can make use of the many forms of electronic media to disseminate your inquiry. Examples might include publication on a school website, intranet, through social media or by setting up a collaborative Wiki or message board to host continuing discussion. It perhaps goes without saying that these media offer interactive ways to reach larger, more diverse audiences but at the same time they demand extra care over issues of anonymity and confidentiality.

Publishing your work

We would encourage you to consider your work for publication in a professional journal. As we pointed out at the start of this chapter, little of the research that teachers read is written by their fellow practitioners. If our experience of working with teachers has taught us anything, it is that there are fascinating, intriguing and inspirational stories about practice in many hundreds of classrooms just waiting to be shared.

Evaluating impact

As we have said above, the real test of your inquiry is the effect that it has and will continue to have on you and on others. It is notoriously hard to judge this but that shouldn't stop you trying to evaluate critically what you and others have learnt as a result of your inquiry. After all, one of the defining characteristics of education is that it is fundamentally forward looking and so finishing an inquiry should actually just be the start of designing the next inquiry.

Drawing it together

- Writing about what matters to you is always easier and the results are generally more powerful. We may have laboured this point in this book, but it is our experience. Think about what bothers you and you are more likely to write with passion and conviction and . . . better.
- Having said that, writing is difficult and you will need to set aside time and energy to write well. Nobody was born a great academic writer: it takes patience and hard work.
- Few if any people ever sit down and write a whole piece in one go. Break down the task. Try to write little bits as you go along, keep a journal, record you ideas on your phone, write on scraps of paper. No writing is bad writing: it all helps; it all makes you a better writer.
- Writing is personal but it is also better shared. Finding somebody to read or talk about your work with will help you express yourself better and more clearly.
- Teachers' ideas are too important not to be shared within their institutions and beyond. Let people know you are inquiring, let them know what you are inquiring into and think about sharing your ideas more widely.
- Enjoy it! Inquiring, writing and presenting is satisfying (in the end!).

References

Altricher, H., Feldman, A., Posch, P. and Somekh, B. (2008) *Teachers Investigate Their Work*. Abingdon: Routledge.

Carr, W. and Kemmis, A. (2005) Staying critical. *Educational Action Research*, Vol. 13, No. 3, pp. 347–58.

Cochran-Smith, M. and Lytle, S. (2009) *Inquiry as Stance: Practitioner Research for the Next Generation*. New York: Teachers College Press.

Menter, I., Elliot, D., Hulme, M., Lewin, J. and Lowden, K. (2011) *A Guide to Practitioner Research in Education*. London: Sage.

Stables, A. (2003) From discrimination to deconstruction: four modulations of criticality in the humanities and social sciences. *Assessment & Evaluation in Higher Education*, Vol. 28, No. 6, pp. 655–72.

Wyse, D. (2007) *The Good Writing Guide for Education Students*. London: Sage.

Index